PORTRAITS OF
CHINA

JEWEL (Yi)

PORTRAITS OF
CHINA

LUNDA HOYLE GILL

TEXT BY COLIN MACKERRAS

UNIVERSITY OF HAWAII PRESS
HONOLULU

This book is dedicated to

Mark Royal Johnson, M.D.
Oklahoma City, Oklahoma

"...you are the Wind beneath my Wings."©

With words, you have kept my feet on the ground
while validating my faith that THE DREAM is possible."
L.H.G.-

First published in the United States of America 1990 by
University of Hawaii Press
2840 Kolowalu Street, Honolulu, Hawaii 96822

Published in Australia by Crawford House Press 1989

Copyright ©1989 Lunda Hoyle Gill
          & Colin Mackerras
Designed and produced by
Crawford House Press
Panorama Avenue, Bathurst. NSW 2795 Australia

Library of Congress Cataloguing-in-Publication Data

Gill, Lunda Hoyle.
   Portraits of China / Lunda Hoyle Gill and Colin Mackerras.
      p.   cm.
   Includes bibliographical references.
   ISBN 0-8248-1292-1 : $49.95
   1. Ethnology--China. 2. China--Ethnic relations. I. Mackerras,
Colin. II. Title.
DS730,G55 1990
305.8'00951--dc20   89-204146
                           CIP

Printed in Hong Kong
10 9 8 7 6 5 4 3 2 1

CONTENTS

DANCING HORSEMEN (Mongolian)

PREFACE

The high value of the book featuring Lunda Hoyle Gill's fifty-six paintings of the Chinese nationalities certainly goes beyond the reproductions. Embodied in those paintings are her friendly feelings and deep love she cherishes towards the Chinese people as well as her worthy endeavor to bridge gaps in mutual understanding between the Chinese people and the American people. I truly believe that apart from the book's undoubted artistic value, which, as I see it, is characterized by a distinct style, aliveness and richness, Lunda Hoyle Gill has brought our two peoples ever closer to each other with her brushes.

My warm congratulations on the publicaton of the book on Lunda Hoyle Gill's fifty-six paintings of the Chinese people.

Han Xu
Ambassador of the People's Republic of China
to the United States of America

FISHERMEN (Han)

FOREWORD

The People's Republic of China is a unitary multi-national state of 9.6 million square kilometres in area. In this broad and far-reaching land fifty-six nationalities live together with a population of about 1 billion. Through their labours, they have brought wasteland under cultivation, increased production, developed a refined culture, and above all with joint efforts have created their country. The Han is the largest nationality with a population of about 936 million which makes up 93.3 per cent of the total population. In the long process of historical development, the Han people have developed close and extensive political and economic relations as well as close cultural exchange with other nationalities. The Han have absorbed traditions of other nationalities which in turn enriched and advanced Han culture.

Besides the Han, there are fifty-five other nationalities, a total of about 67 million people who make up 6.7 per cent of the whole population. Due to their relatively smaller population they are called minority nationalities. These differ greatly in size. The largest is the Zhuang with about 13 million people. While the Hezhen number only about 1400.

The migrations of the nationalities over history have given rise to their characteristically mixed population distribution. Seventy per cent of all countries and cities in China contain people of more than two nationalities. The Hans are spread throughout most of China and their area of concentration is large. Most of the other nationalities also have their areas of concentration different in size, some being spread over a vast area. The overlapping communities of large and small nationalities form an inseparable whole.

After the founding of the People's Republic of China, the system of national oppression that existed for the thousands of years was abolished. A new era of national equality and unity began. The people of all nationalities are the masters of their country. They manage the affairs of the state jointly and on an equal footing. Moreover, areas in which national minorities are concentrated practise national regional autonomy which ensures their equal status and takes account of their special characteristics. Today minority nationalities initiative in participating in the political life of the state and in the realization of the socialist modernization is brought into full play and the unity and cooperation among the various nationalities are constantly enhanced.

In order to introduce China's minority nationalities to their readers some foreign writers depicted them with their gifted pens from various aspects. However, what makes Mrs Hoyle Gill a unique artist in my eyes is the fact that she has been concerned with China's minority nationalities with whom she has come in contact. While the others used their pens, she used her painting brush. She has presented magnificent paintings which give vivid descriptions about the life and culture of the minority people. These paintings composing the main features of this book are really true to life. I am sure, this brilliant contribution will be helpful for promoting understanding and friendship. Particularly the text written by the distinguished Australian scholar, Professor Colin Mackerras will help the readers to know more about the theme of this work.

So, it is indeed a pleasure for me to write a few words for this magnificent work presented by the outstanding artist.

Song Shuhua
Professor
Central Institute for Nationalities, Beijing

ACKNOWLEDGEMENTS

I truly wish I could name everyone who has been good to me and provided assistance when it has been vitally needed. If so, this book would be filled with names, not pictures, but I remember them in my heart and try to complete the circle of giving by helping others when it is my turn to give.

Each painting in the book carries a small piece inside of it of each person that has been part of its creation. I am eternally grateful for the love and friendship of all the people themselves, especially the people who posed for me.

Painting people from cultures around the world would be impossible without the interest and cooperation from the people themselves and from their countries.

I wish to thank my children, Lunda Lucinda Gill and James Gerald Gill, for their love, understanding and patience. They are both strong and resilient, love the cultures of the world as much as I do, believe in the premise of my work, and act as advisors to my life and my work. I love you both.

Thank you to James Russell Gill. It was his original idea that I should visit China in 1981. In addition, I wish to thank this exceptional man for all the invaluable help he gave me during our marriage.

Words can never express my gratitude to my mother, Lucinda B. Hoyle, for her strength and determination. She made me believe I could do anything, that nothing would be impossible if I kept trying. Thank you to my father, Gerald M. Hoyle, an inspiration to me, a true intellect in every sense of the word, stretching my mind to be curious and eager to learn about the world and its people. Love to Edith Thorpe who taught me to see and to Alice Chambers who gave me the backbone to do something about it.

I received faith in my artistic ability from a relative by birth, Karl Godwin, one of the finest artists of the twentieth century. He attained that elusive quality, perfection in a single canvas, over and over again. He has been my ultimate inspiration in art.

Thanks and love go to my cousin Betty Reed, a woman of impeccable integrity, and a sister to me in every way.

I wish to thank the generosity of all the people of China involved in this project. The paintings could not have been created without their inspiration and exceptional cooperation. Special thanks are due to the following

Chinese friends (in alphabetical order):

Han Xu, Ambassador of the People's Republic of China to the United States of America, and his wife, Madame Ge Qiyun; Huan Guo Yi, officer from the Minority Affairs Commission, Yunnan Province; Huang Jiahua, Ambassador to the United Nations; Hui Jing Fang, former head of the Foreign Affairs Office of the Central Institute of Nationalities; Li Guo Shan, former head of the Foreign Affairs Office of the State Ministry Affairs Commission of China; Li Yang Chin; Liu Bing Jiang; Lui Ping, officer from the Sichuan Province Minority Affairs Commission; Ma Ming Ching; Mao Rua, Lian Shan Yi Minority Affairs Commission, Yunnan Province; Meng Shu Dong; Professor Song Shuhua, Central Institute of Nationalities, Beijing; Sui Hui Jiun; Sun Weixue; Tang Xingbo, Consul General in New York; Wang Zicheng, former Minister Counselor (Cultural Affairs) at the Embassy of the People's Republic of China in the United States of America, and his family; Xie Fei; Zhang Jing Chun; Zhang Qi Ren, Foreign Affairs Office of South East Guizhou Province Autonomous Prefecture; General Zhang Wutang, former Defense Attache of the People's Republic of China to the United States of America, and his wife, Madame Zhow Ying; and Zhao Li Jia.

During my second trip to China, the government provided a very special interpreter, Madame Shen You Ling, from the Central Institute of Minority Nationalities, to travel with me. She is a very remarkable woman and very helpful to me. Thank you, Madame Shen, for your superb assistance.

Special thanks go to Yi Zhixin, a student from Beijing who was an invaluable guest in my house for two years while completing his Master's degree. He is an outstanding young man who helped me truly appreciate the fine qualities of the Chinese people.

In addition to my personal desire, the paintings in this book were created for an exhibition in the Smithsonian Institution in Washington D.C. I wish to thank the Secretary of the Smithsonian Institution, Dr Robert McC. Adams for his considerate support, Dr Robert S. Hoffmann for his many kindnesses, and Dr Donald J. Ortner, a notable intellect, for his expert advice and guidance. Applause goes to Madame Ge Qiyun for creating a radiant piece of calligraphy welcoming the public to the exhibition.

British Petroleum produced "China Portraits", a documentary film on my research painting in China. It premiered during the opening reception of the exhibition. My eternal gratitude to all of you at British Petroleum. This is a valuable film, and a copy is now in the archives of the Metropolitan Museum of Art in New York. The quality of the film was absolutely and totally enhanced by the great generosity of the honorable Charlton Heston for his narration of the film. My everlasting thanks to you, Mr Heston.

Special thanks go to Maria Constantino who gave of herself way beyond the call of duty working as my assistant. Particular thanks to Evelyn Weidman for her unending and tireless help. Thanks also go to Barbara Duffield and Ron Crabtree for sharing China with me in 1981. Appreciation to Annette Kaupp for acting on and believing in my abilities. For their unwavering belief in my art from my earliest days as a student in New York, to today, I wish to say thank you from the depths of me to Dr Katherine West and Dr L. Jolyon West, Anne and John.

I must include a very special thank you to my remarkable circle of Oklahoma City friends. One, they taught me how to take risks. Two, they had, and still have, unbelievable faith in my ability and talent. Three, from the first year I met them, these friends have provided a stable rock for me to hang onto when the going got tough. Among these friends are: Mr & Mrs William Beard, Mr & Mrs Fred Hartman, Dr & Mrs Mark R. Johnson, Mr & Mrs John Kirkpatrick, Dr & Mrs William Lockard, Dr & Mrs Thomas Nix, Dr & Mrs William Parry, Mr & Mrs Noel Riggs, and Dr & Mrs Galen Robbins. There are so many more Oklahoma friends that are in my heart; I wish the space were available to name every one of you. You know who you are and know you have my undying love, gratitude and admiration.

In addition, I also wish to thank my remarkable friends in the Washington D.C. area for their faith, original thinking, creativity and help. My love to you all.

Last, but with extreme importance, I give my love and affection to Xin, who is always there when I am in need. You are a vital and essential part of my life.

Lunda Hoyle Gill

ORTHOGRAPHY STATEMENT

In this book we have normally followed the romanization usages of the People's Republic of China. Most minority nationality names have generally accepted spellings there. The officially accepted romanization for standard Chinese in the People's Republic is called *pinyin* and we have adopted it here.

A few very simple rules of pronunciation of the *pinyin* follow.

Vowels:	*a* sounds short *u* as in bun;
	u sounds short *oo* as in book.
Consonants:	*c* sounds *ts* as in hats;
	q sounds *ch* as in chin;
	x sounds *sh* as in she;
	z sounds *dz* like the *ds* in lads;
	zh sounds *j* as in John.
For example	*zhang* sounds like *jung*;
	qing sounds like *ching*;
	han sounds like hun;
	zhou sounds like Joe;
	xi sounds like she.

For historical Tibetan and Mongolian names we have adopted the international systems of romanization which are currently standard, eg. those used in the *Harvard Journal of Asiatic Studies*.

LIST OF PLATES

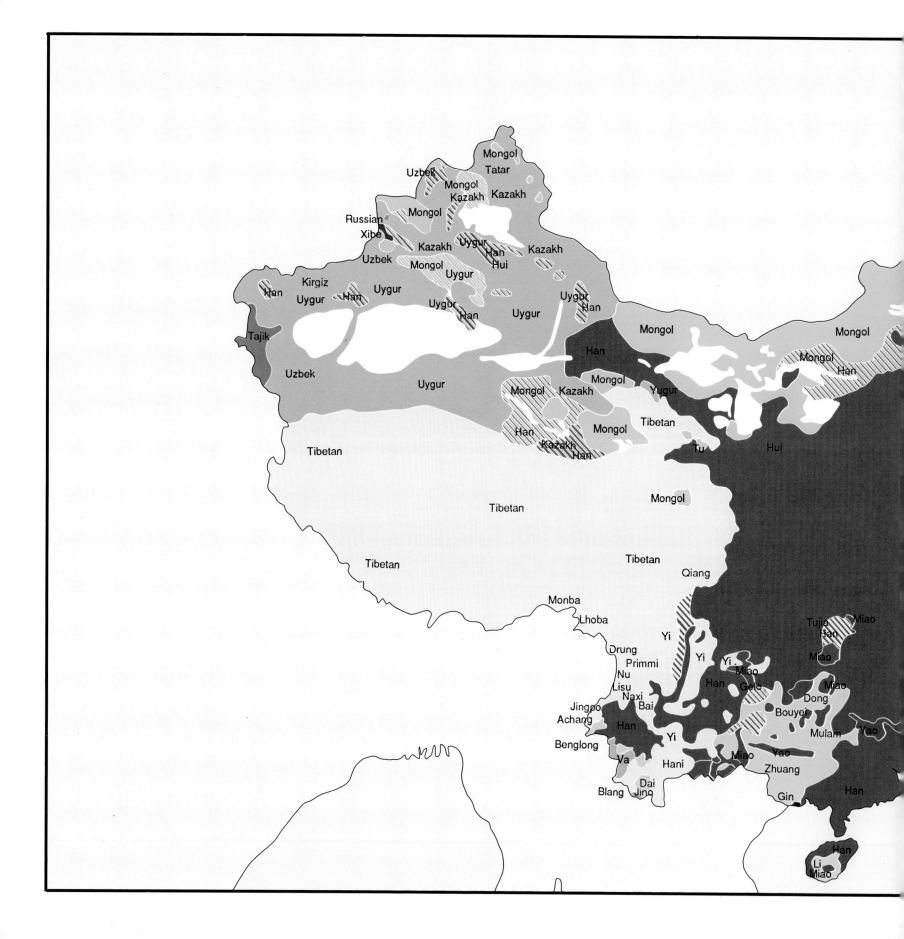

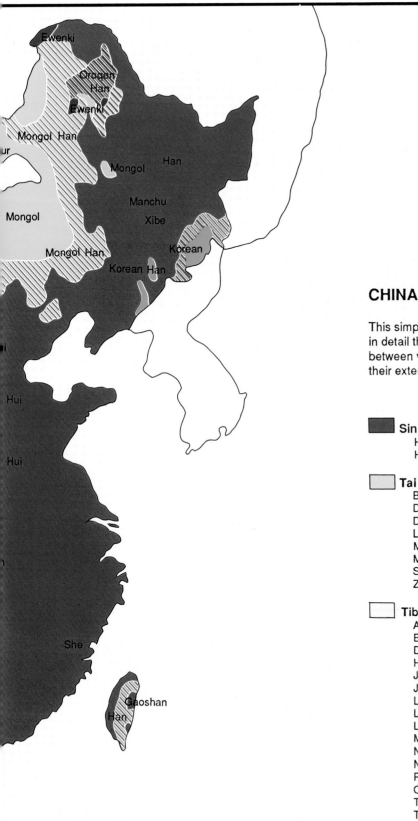

CHINA'S NATIONALITIES

This simple map indicates by color, China's language families. It does not show in detail the full distribution of the minority nationalities nor the extent of overlap between various nationalities, however, their location is indicated by type, but not their extent.

Sinitic
Han
Hui

Tai
Bouyei
Dai
Dong
Li
Maonan
Mulam
Sui
Zhuang

Tibeto-Burman
Achang
Bai
Drung
Hani
Jingpo
Jino
Lahu
Lisu
Lhoba
Monba
Naxi
Nu
Primmi
Qiang
Tibetan
Tujia
Yi

Miao-Yao
Gelo
Miao
She
Yao

Turkic
Kazakh
Kirgiz
Salar
Tatar
Uygur
Uzbek
Yugur

Mongol
Bonan
Daur
Dongxiang
Mongol
Tu

Tungus-Manchu
Ewenki
Hezhen
Manchu
Oroqen
Xibe

Korean
Korean

Malayo-Polynesian
Gaoshan

Mon-Khmer
Benglong
Blang
Va

Vietnamese
Gin

Iranian
Tajik

Slavic
Russian

Uninhabited

JESTER (Yi)

NOTES BY THE ARTIST

CHINA - the word itself brings visions of beauty and mystery. Many of us, when we think of China, think about her many treasures, art, land and architecture, but her real treasure is in her one billion people. They are industrious, polite, eager, full of curiosity, and proud of their identity.

For many years, I have had a compelling urge to paint people before their individual beauty is lost forever to encroaching change, to capture a little of their dignity and inner richness and to touch their subtle core of life; I wish to paint the people as they are now. I am obsessed with the desire to record as many of the surviving cultures as possible. It is inevitable that tradition will change as technology creeps into their lives. I am not asking that technology be stopped, but I am asking to be a part of this program to record, and hence, preserve, man's national heritage.

When I paint in the field, there is only a small instant of time to capture the inner essence of a living soul. I must become aware of every nuance, every movement, every thought that crosses their faces. It gives me such joy to observe every detail of their wrinkles, tone, color and intensity of skin; observe how coarse or fine the hair is, how the head rests on the shoulders, what the hands say. I observe every inner and outer aspect of the physical image and at the same time, pay special attention to the inner self. In addition, I wish to tell their cultural story through their dress or environment while never losing sight that the dress and the environment are of secondary importance. The pure beauty of the people I paint lies in their inner self - here is where the essence of life dwells. This core is where the universality of man comes together. Here is where we realize we are all alike; where we have common elements of life, such as wishing for a better life for our children and grandchildren, feeling joy and experiencing pain, sharing love with another, aching to have peace in our lifetime. Yes, we are alike in so many ways - we are human.

What tremendous joy I find in looking at a new blank canvas - painting the person before me. All of a sudden that person comes "alive" before me and winks! I can't begin to describe this feeling in words. Many times I have slept under the stars, dreaming about the very special beauty I will experience the next day - the person who will sit for me - I am so excited by what I will see and be fortunate enough to paint. I thank the stars and say how lucky I am, lucky to meet other cultures, share their lives and create a painting of them that will last long after we are gone.

With great awe I stepped through the entrance into the Forbidden City in Beijing. This one step carried me back through thousands of years of history. I hoped the gods would not be too angry as we swarmed over past sacred ground. Instead, a touching, sensitive experience occurred. After viewing the palaces and grounds I entered the Imperial Garden and saw a beautiful baby who was touring with his parents. I asked if I could take his picture. This pleased the parents; they were so proud of him. They said, "Yes." He was so beautiful I took many pictures. I will never forget what occurred next. The mother took all the boy's clothes off and said with her eyes, "There, see what a perfect and beautiful son I have." Yes, he was so beautiful and perfect in every way. A Chinese couple standing near us watching this whole occurrence said, "These people must live in the country as this is an old custom with country people to show the perfection of a child. The parents take pride in showing he is a boy." What a loving and open experience this was.

After returning to Hong Kong from the twelve-day tour in 1981, my desire was to reenter China with my art supplies and to start painting the people immediately. Very few people were traveling independently in China at this time. I knew it would be hard to acquire the permit to reenter as an individual, but we were fortunate and received the permission. This was truly exciting news. The Government was also gracious in including my son, Jim, and a Canadian couple, Barbara Duffield and Ron Crabtree whom we had met on the twelve-day tour, to accompany me. They were wonderful to travel with - a great help in every way. We will always have a special bond of friendship because of this trip.

It was very hard getting permission (and I am so grateful for this permission) to travel to Tibet during this time to paint the Tibetans. I visited the Joh Hang Temple and saw a superb, dignified, older Tibetan man. His face was marked by the history of Tibet. The true beauty in his face told me I had to paint him so I grabbed this man by the arm and sent Jim to get the interpreter. Here I was holding onto this man with him not knowing what in the world I was doing! When my interpreter finally arrived we were faced with another dilemma! She only spoke Han and the man whose arm I was still holding only spoke Tibetan. We needed to find a Tibetan interpreter so that I could explain to this man why I wouldn't let him go! If eyes can speak louder than words, he was truly speaking with his loudest, most suspicious eyes. By this time there was a crowd of people surrounding us. The Tibetan interpreter finally arrived and, after much talk, the man agreed to sit for a painting. The Tibetans are so intriguing to me. This man's face looked as if it was carved out of the Himalayas, appearing to be a stone lantern with a light inside.

After working and traveling in south China and Tibet, we were on our way to Inner Mongolia from Chengdu with a change of trains in Lanzhou. While waiting for the train to Inner Mongolia, another train was preparing to go to Urumqi in northwest China. We all looked at each other, grabbed our bags and off we went on another adventure to Urumqi, Turpan, and the Old Silk Road. The people I painted there are Muslim and are closer to Arabs in appearance with strong, angular faces. Mongolia could wait! We did continue, however, to Mongolia and I had the good fortune to paint a Mongolian bride in all her finery; necklaces and a headpiece made of silver, turquoise and bright, red beads. The jewelry had been passed down in the family for generations.

This individual trip through China, though arduous, was one of the truly great times of my life: beauty to paint, adventures to experience, lessons to learn from a very ancient culture and the sharing of this with my son and two friends. My only regret was that my daughter, Lundy, was still in school and not able to be part of this adventure. She has traveled with me before and will again in the future.

In 1984 I returned to China to continue my painting. By this time the Chinese government was aware of my interest in painting their people and provided invaluable help including plans for my travel, logistics and research. I had total freedom in the areas I wished to cover. The local officials worked closely with me in locating traditional subjects that needed to be put on canvas. The government is vitally interested in the preservation of the various minority cultures. This greatly impressed me. By this time too, arrangements had been established to exhibit the paintings in the Smithsonian Institution, Washington D.C. in 1986. With this in mind I paid special attention to the research work that has always accompanied each of my paintings. The Chinese government provided an exceptional interpreter to travel with me - Shen You Ling. Shen, a highly intelligent, creative and perceptive woman close to my own age, provided support. She will forever be my Chinese sister. Having previously worked in China alone with no assistance and not speaking the language I was tremendously grateful for her help. She was instrumental in acquiring the factual information needed to accompany the individual paintings. I must have personal information about subjects as well as information about the group or nationality he or she is representing.

Painting in the field is always challenging and exciting. One day I would paint on a porch, the next day under the shade of a tree with my canvas propped against a rock. I am usually the entertainment for the village. Children and adults alike would watch me. Even small fingers would find their way into my paints and sometimes another brush would be mysteriously painting on my canvas with me! Each sitting takes from two to five hours, during which I make a detailed oil portrait on canvas of the person's head and a rough sketch of the body. The painting is finished back home in my studio. I keep careful notes of colors, textures and artifacts that will aid the final painting. My paintings rarely have backgrounds. The focus is on the person's face and eyes. My whole being strives to record the depth of the inner person, as well as the outer physical likeness.

Another amazing experience occurred in Inner Mongolia. If you were in Inner Mongolia who would be the most exciting person you could think of meeting? A person you could share many hours of talk over a Mongolian hot pot, talking late into the night about ancient stories and feats of dangerous horsemanship? Ghengis Khan. Well of course I did not meet the man himself, but miracles of miracles, I ate breakfast with the next best individual, Ghengis Khan's twenty-third descendant. I couldn't believe it! He and his wife wished to share his great joy that day. He was going to visit the grave of his ancestor. He had left Inner Mongolia forty years before as a small child and this was the first time he had returned. I was mesmerized by this. Later that day I visited the museum in Hohhot and looked at the stone embodiment of the "man" I met at breakfast. The plaque under the bust said "Ghengis Khan". How could that same steel be in his ancestor's eyes after twenty-three generations?

Working in the field is pure joy. It is the relationship I have with the people I meet and paint that excites me. The exhilaration I feel painting people in their own environment is indescribable.

The people were very pleased to be painted and eager to tell me about their life experiences and customs. I have been blessed by the people who have posed for me. One of my greatest worries in undertaking this work was how people would accept my desire to paint them. However, the Chinese were patient and giving.

At first they are very shy and reserved not knowing what is going to happen to them. I don't let the person see the painting until I am finished.

While I paint I must totally isolate my mind and eyes and devote all my senses to the subject and the painting. I must totally block out the rest of the world. The two of us are bonded together in a human chrysalis; I feel the person sitting for me is painting through my eyes and my hands. I am only there to guide the brush and capture the moment. When the painting, which is only a research painting, is finished, I turn it around for the subject to see. I then ask the subject to sign his or her name and group on the canvas.

After bringing home the research paintings I begin the new canvas. These paintings can have a variance in size from 10" x 12" to 60" x 48". The subject tells my mind what size would work best for that particular painting.

All of us can be proud of our own particular cultural heritage, and as my Chinese friends move into the 21st century, I hope they will cherish and be proud of theirs. I hope their pride will be enhanced by the fact that a stranger saw rare beauty in their souls and in their culture. When viewing my paintings I trust that you will like my friends and feel a little closer to them. Maybe this is truly what art is all about: communication between people.

My admiration and respect for my Chinese friends will be with them forever.

THREE DANCERS (Mongolian)

INTRODUCTION

I n terms of population China is the world's first and only billion-aire. A census taken in mid-1982 showed just over 1,000 million people in those territories currently governed from Beijing, that is, not including Taiwan or Hong Kong.

These billion or so people belong to fifty-six nationalities. The largest is called Han and has been so since about the time of Christ. In 1982 it took up 93.3 per cent of the population and is thus the one most readily associated with China, even though a sample census in 1987 showed the proportion had dropped to 92 per cent.

The other 6.7 or 8 per cent are the fifty-five minority nationalities. They may be few relative to the Han, but they still accounted for over 85 million people in 1987. Even without the Han, they would make China among the more populous countries on earth.

What is a nationality? The definition adopted in contemporary China is very close to Stalin's. It sees a nationality as a historically constituted stable community of people with a common territory, a common language, a common economic life and a common culture (Chen 1987:344).

The main aim of this general survey is to provide background on the general histories, languages, economies, and cultures of China's minority nationalities, in order to assist in the appreciation of the magnificent paintings which form the core of this book. The term "culture" is taken to include religion, courtship and marriage, literature, and the arts.

In dealing with the relationships between a majority nationality and the minorities in any country, social scientists use a range of concepts to analyse the extent to which the former influences and dominates the latter. On the liberal end of the spectrum are ideas such as pluralism, which suggests a high degree of freedom for the minorities. At the other extreme is assimilation, according to which the minorities move towards losing their identity altogether and simply becoming absorbed into the majority. Part of the aim of this survey is to comment on where Chinese policy and reality lies along this spectrum in the late years of the twentieth century.

1. HISTORY

The origins of the Chinese people are shrouded in mystery. Probably, however, the influence of minority nationalities in the foundation of Chinese culture is greater than traditional Han historians have acknowledged. These tended to assume that the Han people originated in the Yellow River Valley in Central China and spread outwards, absorbing the 'barbarians', endowing upon them the blessings of Han civilization. Within the borders of what is now China there have lived since time immemorial peoples of various cultures, speaking different languages and with a variety of ways of producing what they need to live, in short different nationalities. Rather than postulating a dominant people which spread to absorb the others, it may be preferable to see mutual cultural influences leading to a Chinese civilization varying in some respects from region to region and bearing the traits of nationalities which have become assimilated into the Han people. Over history many nationalities have indeed ceased to exist as separate entities, and become part of the Han.

On the other hand, many of China's surviving minority nationalities have histories going back well before the time of Christ. The ancestors of the Yao and Miao nationalities of the southwest of China have been identified with 'barbarian' peoples mentioned in historical works referring to the third century BC. Even earlier are the forebears of the Manchus of the northeast, references in Chinese historical books dating back as far as the eleventh century BC.

Clearly the relationships between these minority peoples on the one hand, and the Han Chinese on the other, are a very important feature of China's history. The Han Chinese feared invasion from their northern neighbours from very early times, hence the Great Wall, completed from unconnected sections under the great but tyrannical ruler Qin Shihuang (reigned 246 BC-210 BC), China's first unifier. Despite this, northern China was indeed many times ruled by foreign powers. Twice in its history, the whole of China has been overwhelmed by foreign peoples to its north, once by the Mongols, who unified China under their Yuan dynasty (1280-1368), and once by the Manchus, who established the Qing dynasty (1644-1911).

The people who conquered north China were often assimilated by the Han. A case in point is the Xianbei people, who ruled most of northern China from 386 AD for a century and a half. Of the two peoples who overwhelmed the whole of China, the Mongols were not assimilated and even today many of them live in their own independent Mongolian People's Republic. The Manchus are still classified as a minority nationality, but have been integrated by the Han Chinese to an extent far greater than the Mongols. They have, for instance, given up their written and spoken languages almost entirely and now use Chinese.

The Han Chinese have on many occasions throughout history taken over areas in which non-Chinese people resided. Qin Shihuang not only unified China but also increased its area by conquering areas inhabited by non-Chinese peoples. The territory ruled by the Chinese government has greatly increased since then, including areas which are the home of non-Chinese peoples. However, the process has not been consistent. Thus the empire of the Tang (618-907 AD) included, at least in the first half, the area now called Xinjiang in the far west of China. The succeeding Song dynasty (960-1279) was much smaller in extent. Under the Yuan dynasty, China was part of Mongolia rather than the converse, but in any case the extent of the khanate of the Great Khan was vast, encompassing all of Tibet, Mongolia and Manchuria, as well as Korea and other places. It was during the Mongol period that Yunnan province, with its many minority nationalities, was absorbed permanently into China. However, Xinjiang belonged to a separate khanate from China. Cultural and social interchange between Han and minority nationalities was cumulatively extensive over the centuries. Influence ran in both directions. Many features of what is nowadays regarded as Chinese culture take their origin from customs practised by minority nationalities dwelling inside or near the Chinese empire. But influence the other way was much more pervasive, that is to say, processes of assimilation or integration have tended to favour Han culture rather than those of the minorities. These have taken over more from the Han than the other way round.

A central reason for this was the spread of the Han method of agriculture. Administration in imperial China came from walled cities which were garrisoned by Han Chinese troops, including in the areas remote from the capital and near the frontier where the local population might belong to a minority nationality. Han peasants tended to follow the troops, either voluntarily or otherwise, and established their own system of farming, with its irrigation techniques, iron tools, and manuring methods. The Han were usually able to produce more from the land than the minorities, who were often not agriculturalists anyway, but pastoralists.

Han Chinese rule could be rather indirect. From the Yuan and Ming (1368-1644) dynasties on, for example, non-Han border areas of Yunnan were placed under a system by which the Chinese government granted local chieftains authority, calling them *tusi*. As long as these local power-holders sent revenue to the capital, secured in any way they wished, the government left them alone to rule their own areas as they pleased.

This policy of neglect was in no way benign. It meant that the minority nationalities could be segregated and ignored, except when the government or officials needed the money or produce of the ordinary person. Above all, its result was that nobody was either able or willing to prevent the most ferocious exploitation of the poor by the rich at the lowest levels of society.

China's history includes many peasant rebellions against the government and officials, a natural response to the hard life and exploitation suffered by the peasants. It is not surprising to find the minorities involved in these rebellions. From the Han dynasty (206 BC-220 AD) to the early Qing there were over a dozen major rebellions in which minority nationalities took part, either alone or in cooperation with Han peasants. In the Song dynasty, for instance, the Miao, Yao and Dong people in southern China joined with Han peasants in killing officials. A rebellion of the Yao nationality spanned almost all the Ming dynasty, flaring up periodically from 1375 to 1627. Its overall effects were catastrophic for the Yao, since it brought in its wake military occupation, destruction of villages and towns, and slaughter on a scale sufficient to cause a sharp decline in the population of the Yao (Yaozu: 53-61).

Yet it would be a mistake to see the non-Han peoples as always against the government of China. A very important illustrative example is that of the Uygurs in the mid-eighth century. The Tang dynasty was shaken from 755 to 763 by a rebellion led initially by An Lushan, the largest in scale of the medieval Chinese rebellions. The Uygurs at the time controlled their own independent empire centred on what is now Mongolia. They sent troops to aid the Tang against the An Lushan rebellion and played a decisive role in its suppression. Without Uygur help, the Tang might possibly have been overthrown. In 762 the ruler of the Uygurs went himself to China to lead his troops against the rebels.

The example highlights the fact that a minority nationality of China in one era is a foreign people in another. China's history is so long and vast that the ancestors of more or less all the minority nationalities of today at one time lived beyond China's borders. The Uygurs of the eighth century did not regard themselves as Chinese subjects, whatever the Chinese court may have thought.

In terms of its extent, the Qing dynasty forms a high point of the imperial age. In the eighteenth century the Manchus extended their power westward and secured overlordship in Tibet. By 1759 they had also conquered Turkestan. The Manchu policy was to posit five equal nationalities: Manchus, Han, Mongols, Tibetans and Moslems. Certainly, however, the five were not equal, since the Manchus held the government reins and the Han were the most populous.

The nationalities continued to see themselves as exploited. The nineteenth century witnessed numerous rebellions. The Zhuang, Yao and other peoples of the south and southwest took part in the Taiping revolution of 1851 to 1864. There were several very large-scale rebellions by Moslem peoples. In particular, in the far west, Yakub Beg led the Uygurs and others in an attempt to detach Turkestan from China. The Manchu court sent troops against him and waged a long, expensive and bloody but eventually successful war to retain control over the area. The victory came in 1877 and was followed, late in 1884, by the formal establishment of Turkestan as the Chinese province of Xinjiang, which means literally 'new border'. The wounds and resentments by the Uygurs against the Han lasted long after that time.

It was during this period that the Korean nationality in China came into existence, due to migration. Korea was a tributary state of China's until 1895. Although a small number of Koreans had moved to China as early as the late seventeenth century, the impetus for major migration was a serious famine in northern Korea in 1869. When Korea became a Japanese colony in 1910, expatriate Koreans in China organized raids across the Sino-Korean border against the Japanese regime, which, for its part, undertook very extensive migration of Koreans out of their own country, including to Manchuria. There were also Koreans who fled to Manchuria to escape Japanese oppression.

The late Qing and Republican period in China was an extremely unstable one. In 1910 Qing troops occupied Tibet. The British attempted from India to influence developments in Tibet and at the Simla Conference of 1913-1914 reached an agreement with the local Tibetan regime under which Outer Tibet, including the capital Lhasa, would become independent of China, while Inner Tibet, the region nearer Sichuan province, would remain under a Chinese and Tibetan government. No Chinese government has ever recognized, let alone signed, the Simla Agreement. In 1942, under British influence, the Tibetan regime set up a Foreign Affairs Bureau, signalling independence from China. The Chinese government protested but was powerless against the strong British influence exerted from India.

Xinjiang likewise became effectively independent for a time, though not formally so. In the 1930s, the Han Chinese Sheng Shicai established a radical socialist regime there and in April 1934 proclaimed his 'Six Great Principles', which included friendship with the Soviet Union and anti-imperialism. However, he quarrelled with the Soviets and in 1942 ordered all Russians, including military advisers, to leave Xinjiang. He then submitted to Chiang Kaishek.

At least part of Mongolia opted not only for effective but total and formal independence of China. Military attempts by the Beijing governments to prevent the disintegration of Chinese control in Mongolia proved unsuccessful; and the Soviet Union assisted the Mongolian Communists in the establishment of the Mongolian People's Republic, the first long-lasting socialist state in Asia, in the region which the Chinese called Outer Mongolia. The constitution formally proclaiming the Mongolian People's Republic was adopted in November 1924. Chiang Kaishek's Nationalist regime did not recognize the independence of

Outer Mongolia until August 1945.

Chiang Kaishek's government followed the Qing in declaring five nationalities in China: Han, Manchus, Mongols, Tibetans and Moslems. It included a Mongolian and Tibetan Affairs Commission. However, it did not formulate an overall coherent policy on nationalities until the end of 1946, when the Constitution of the Republic of China laid down equality for all and proper representation for the minority nationalities in the governing bodies of China. By 1946 it was too late for effective action by Chiang's regime and the provisions of the Constitution on nationalities were never properly implemented.

The Chinese Communist Party (CCP) had, meanwhile, begun to work out a policy on nationalities, based on ideas coming from the Soviet Union. The CCP set up its Chinese Soviet Republic, with Ruijin in Jiangxi Province as its capital, in November 1931. At the same time, the Constitution of the Republic was proclaimed. In its Article 14 it recognized the right of the minority nationalities to choose separation and independence from China (CK,V, 453):

> All Mongolians, Hui, Tibetans, Miao, Li, Koreans
> and others living within the territory of China enjoy
> the full right of self-determination, that is, they may
> either secede from the Union of Chinese Soviets or set
> up their own autonomous region.

The Long March of 1934-1935, which followed the destruction of the Chinese Soviet Republic at the hands of Chiang Kaishek's troops, brought the CCP forces from Jiangxi to northern Shaanxi, where they made their headquarters in Yan'an. The route took the Red Army through many minority nationality areas. On the whole, the CCP's soldiers treated the minorities well and certainly gained recruits for their cause. The famous American journalist Edgar Snow reports (1972: 451) that there were Mongols, Moslems, Tibetans, Miao and Yi among the students working in Yan'an. He also notes (pp. 356-361) the existence of Red Moslem regiments with quite well developed class consciousness. Communist Moslem soldiers told him that they regarded the Han Chinese as brothers in a common revolution and denied that the Red Army interfered with Moslem worship.

The CCP made a point of uniting with the minority nationalities against the Japanese during the war. This was natural because two of their main base areas in north China contained territory inhabited by the Mongols. As early as 1935 Mao Zedong had claimed (I, 161) that the minority nationalities, especially the people of Inner Mongolia, were 'rising up in struggle' because of the direct menace of Japanese imperialism. As it turned out, the Inner Mongolian Autonomous Region, headed by the well-known Mongolian Communist leader Ulanhu, was set up on 1 May 1947, that is, more than two years before the establishment of the People's Republic of China itself.

2. POLICY

The accession of the CCP to power brought quick and dramatic changes in attitudes towards the minority nationalities. In September 1949, just before the formal establishment of the People's Republic of China (PRC) on 1 October, a united front body consisting of the CCP and various other groups allied with it adopted the Common Programme. This document became, and remains, the basis of the various Chinese Constitutions and was the first formal statement of the new regime's policies. Chapter VI of the Common Programme, Articles 50-53, spells out policy on the nationalities.

Article 50 reads:

> All nationalities within the boundaries of the People's Republic of China are equal. They shall establish unity and mutual aid among themselves and shall oppose imperialism and their own public enemies, so that the People's Republic of China will become a big fraternal and cooperative family composed of all its nationalities. Greater nationalism and chauvinism shall be opposed. Acts involving discrimination, oppression and splitting of the unity of the various nationalities shall be prohibited.

This statement is summed up in the slogan 'unity and equality' which has remained the ideal throughout the history of the PRC. Few people claim it as reality, but the extent to which it falls short has varied considerably from period to period.

It is striking that there is no reference to the right to secede, which had been incorporated into the CCP's 1931 Constitution. China is to be a multinational unitary state in which all nationalities within its borders are equal but certainly may not secede. Attempts to incite secession are no doubt among the crimes which the framers of the Common Programme had in mind in their reference to opposing 'imperialism and their own public enemies'.

In opposition to secession, the Common Programme outlined a right of regional autonomy for the minority nationalities. What this means is that in any area of concentration of particular nationalities, they may set up governments exercising authority autonomously from the central government. There are several levels, the highest being the autonomous region, which is equivalent to a province. There are five autonomous regions in China, the Inner Mongolian, the Xinjiang Uygur, the Guangxi Zhuang, the Ningxia Hui and the Tibetan. The last four were set up, respectively, in October 1955, March 1958, October 1958, and September 1965.

Autonomy is by no means a sham. It gives the nationality governments rights to pass certain laws which are different from those of the PRC, provided the central government agrees. Concrete examples are that some of the nationality areas allow marriage at a younger age than 20 for women, 22 for men, which are prescribed under the PRC Marriage Law of September 1980. The current policy that married couples in general produce no more than one child specifically exempts the minority nationalities, most of which allow two but impose a fine for a third. Another aspect of autonomy is that, by law, the different nationalities dwelling within the autonomous areas must be appropriately and properly represented in the local organs of political power.

On the other hand, autonomy is not independence and does not pretend to be. The need for the central government to approve local laws places restrictions on what autonomous authorities can do. Moreover, there are no autonomous parties and it is the CCP which is the main power-wielder in China. There is only one Chinese Communist Party and no autonomous branches for any nationality, whether Han, Uygur, Korean or Tibetan.

The Common Programme gave the minority nationalities two other important rights. The first one was the right to join the People's Liberation Army and to organize local public security forces. This has not prevented Han soldiers from entering nationality areas, especially Xinjiang and Tibet.

The other right is the freedom to use their own languages, and to follow their own traditions, customs and religious beliefs. According to Article 53 of the Common Programme, the Chinese government must help the minority nationalities 'to develop their political, economic, cultural, and educational construction work'. These rights are not absolute and some of them may conflict with PRC law. For instance, some of the minority nationalities are Moslems, whose traditions allow a plurality of wives, whereas PRC law prescribes no more than one. Certainly the right to follow tradition does not extend to polygamy. The Va people of southwest Yunnan Province used to offer sacrifices of a severed human head in the belief that the blood would procure a good harvest. Obviously the PRC government was not prepared to allow head-hunting sacrifices simply because it was the tradition of a minority nationality.

One of the first tasks of the new government was to decide precisely which groups constituted nationalities under the definition proposed by Stalin, which has itself never been seriously challenged in official PRC government circles. In 1953 Chinese social scientists began field work to try and reach a verdict on some 400 names claimed as separate nationalities. By the time of the 1964 census fifty-four independent ethnic groups had received official recognition. Yet many people still wished to be regarded as belonging to a minority nationality, which itself speaks well of the acceptance of CCP policy at that time. In the census, which asked household heads to specify their family's nationality, there were claims of no less than 183 different nationalities, far below 400 but well above the official figure of the time. Since then only one further nationality has been added to the official list, namely the Juno (Jinuo in Chinese) of Yunnan Province, accepted by the State Council as a nationality in June 1979. Efforts persist to define particular groups as separate nationalities or otherwise, but as of 1989 there are fifty-six officially recognized nationalities in China, the Han and fifty-five minorities.

To apply a uniform policy to these fifty-five groups has not been easy. Some of them differ sharply from each other and the Han, others less so. The Zhuang of Guangxi, China's most populous minority nationality, and some others are very well integrated with the Han and in most respects not too different from them. On the other hand, the Uygurs are ethnically Turkic, believe in Islam and have a culture which is very much closer to that of the Turks than to the Han Chinese. Some degree of autonomy is only sensible in persuading diverse peoples to live together in harmony with each other and the Han.

Within this autonomy, the Common Programme's demand that the government should 'assist' all nationalities has remained a permanent feature of PRC policy. But help can easily be construed as paternalistic, because it may imply that the helping group is superior to that assisted and is the one determining just what kind of aid is needed. Does assistance by the government to all nationalities in fact mean that the Han tell the minorities what to do, calling it help? Certainly in all periods many Han cadres have taken such an attitude, or at least behaved as if they did. Moreover, many official statements have declared, as the then PRC Central Government Deputy Chairman Liu Shaoqi did in his report on the draft Constitution in September 1954, that 'for historical reasons the Han nationality has a comparatively higher political, economic, and cultural level than the others', and thus must help the more 'backward' nationalities.

On the other hand, Liu Shaoqi specifically denied that the Han were entitled to any special privileges or 'to put on airs towards its brother nationalities'. Moreover, in 1955 Mao Zedong (V, 169), Chairman of the CCP from 1935 till his death in 1976, denounced the notion that help was one-way. He argued, in fact, that the Han had given the minority nationalities 'little help and in some places no help at all' and went on to say that the minority nationalities, on the other hand, had 'rendered help to the Hans'. The 1982 PRC Constitution is among numerous documents requiring 'mutual assistance' between the various nationalities, whether Han or minority.

The goals of this mutual assistance are supposed to be socialist and hence common to all nationalities. They include stability, industrialization, universal education, good health delivery systems, and social harmony. In some of these the Han may well be leaders, though it should be pointed out that the Mongolians had already established a socialist state when the CCP was still small, young and weak. The Han are by no means the only Chinese nationality with interest in establishing industry. Yet it remains true that some of the minorities knew more or less nothing of such modern phenomena as industry when the CCP came to power. To exclude them from a modernizing process simply because it lay outside their tradition and they did not ask for it, would be far more paternalistic than to encourage them to advance, along with all other nationalities, towards a common modernized future.

The question of mutual help relates closely to the central problem of relations among the nationalities of China, the dichotomy between great Han chauvinism and local nationalism. The former is that ill by which the Han regard themselves as superior to other nationalities and treat them as overlords do a subject race. Local nationalism means the tendency of minority nationality leaders to seek secession from China or in other ways defy the overall leadership of the CCP. Both are inimical to national unity.

The history of the PRC can be seen in terms of attempts by the central government to uproot both evils, with the emphasis now on one, now on the other. In general, the more radical phases, especially the Great Leap Forward (1958-1960) and the Cultural Revolution (1966-1976), attacked local nationalism more severely, while the others, above all the years since 1980, have hit hardest at great Han chauvinism.

The early and mid-1950s were a hopeful period in the application of the PRC policies towards the minority nationalities. The first of the PRC Constitutions, that of 1954, followed the Common Programme very closely. The standard of living rose sharply in nationality areas in response to the government's despatch of relief teams, medical aid and food. It was government policy that the nationalities might achieve socialism at different rates from the Han and each other, according to local conditions. The minorities were impressed by what looked like the first real attempt in China's history to give them a fair deal.

By late 1957, however, relations began to deteriorate. The Great Leap Forward saw an attempt to speed up Mao's vision of socialization everywhere in China and effective withdrawal of certain exemptions which the minority nationalities had enjoyed.

The most serious incident to affect the minorities in these years was a full-scale rebellion in Tibet. The region had been formally incorporated into the PRC in 1951, but the old social system had been left more or less unchanged. The Dalai Lama attended the First National People's Congress in 1954 and chaired a Preparatory Committee set up to plan the establishment of the Tibetan Autonomous Region.

In March 1959 an organized Tibetan army rose up against the

Chinese government. The Dalai Lama and his followers saw the Tibetan people and culture as under threat of destruction and their country as being made a mere appendage of China. Some years later Dawa Norbu, a vocal Tibetan refugee, wrote (1974: 213) that 'Tibet is no longer a country; it is a mere geographical expression'. He went on to complain that the people's 'labour and natural resources are exploited for the glory of China and the Hans. In short, the Chinese Communists are milking Tibet as well as the Tibetans'.

The Chinese government denied Tibet had any right to be called a 'country'. It claimed the revolt was led by members of the old ruling classes, lamas and other land-owning aristocrats, and was backed by active American support. Chris Mullin (1975: 30-34) has produced very strong evidence in support of the last contention, and claimed that the Dalai Lama himself confirmed the main points of his argument. In particular, Mullin alleges that the American Central Intelligence Agency parachuted guns and trained guerrillas into Tibet from 1957 to 1961, and that early in 1958 the Americans tried to persuade the Dalai Lama's regime to appeal openly for US intervention.

In the event the uprising was quickly put down by the Chinese army with considerable bloodshed. The Dalai Lama fled to India, followed by a large number of refugees. The Tibetans who had opposed the rebellion helped the Chinese army re-establish political control. Reforms were carried out which uprooted the old social system.

Although the early 1960s saw a general return to milder treatment of the nationalities, the Cultural Revolution decade which followed was the most assimilative period in the history of the PRC so far. The doctrine of the Cultural Revolution was that the 'key link' in all matters was class struggle. As far as the minority nationalities were concerned, this meant that problems must be seen in terms of class, and not culture, let alone race. Tibetan or Zhuang peasants were thus the allies of the Han peasants against Tibetan, Zhuang or Han feudal remnants. This obscured very real racial tensions and merely inflamed the minority nationalities.

Han Red Guards were sent into the nationality areas to try and overthrow local rulers, virtually all of whom they denounced for local

POLICY

nationalism. Saifudin, the Uygur leader of Xinjiang, and Ulanhu of Inner Mongolia, both of whom had been loyal to the PRC, were among those thrown out of office. The power struggles which took place everywhere during the Cultural Revolution were marked by serious violence, especially in some of the minority areas. A clear symbol of the extreme resistance which the proponents of the Cultural Revolution experienced in the nationality areas was the fact that the last two of the province-level revolutionary committees or new-style radical governments to be established were in Xinjiang and Tibet, both set up on 5 September 1968.

The crime of the Cultural Revolution's followers was to force the minority nationalities to behave like the Han. Many I met in Inner Mongolia, Tibet and Xinjiang complained that Red Guards had suppressed their religion and culture, had forbidden them to perform their own music and dances, and forced unwanted Han revolutionary operas on them. For a time the Cultural Revolution even attempted to suppress the use of minority nationality languages.

Mao Zedong's death in September 1976 and the fall of his main supporters, the 'gang of four', the following month led on to criticism of their policies. In June 1981 the CCP formally and thoroughly denounced the Cultural Revolution as an unmitigated disaster. Meanwhile it had demoted class struggle and declared that its Marxist ideology saw class and nationality as two quite separate matters. The Party's main mouthpiece, the *People's Daily*, wrote on 15 July 1980:

> Nationalities and classes have their own laws governing their emergence, development and extinction. In most cases, the various nationalities....came into being after a history of several hundred or several thousand years, and will continue to exist for a long time to come.... The existence of classes is of much shorter duration than that of nationalities. After the withering away of the former, the latter will remain in existence for a long time.

In accordance with this changed evaluation of the Cultural Revolution and class struggle, the emphasis changed back from attacking local nationalism to denouncing great Han chauvinism. Autonomy for the

15

minority nationalities received far better implementation than at any time before, probably better than the early 1950s. The traditions, religions and arts of the nationalities have revived with greater strength than ever.

One particularly important aspect of this change in policy is a renewed attempt to hand over power in the minority areas to members of the relevant nationalities themselves. Already in 1950s the government had tried to train cadres of the nationalities, for instance by setting up nationalities' institutes. Edgar Snow (1961: 597) reported that in 1961 CCP membership among the minorities exceeded 250,000, that is about 1.5 per cent of the total, as against their 6 per cent of the entire population. Official figures claimed a substantial rise in the number of cadres belonging to the minority nationalities between 1978 and 1982, the proportion of all cadres rising from 4.8 to 5.4 per cent. The trend is in the right direction, though this last figure is still below the 6.7 per cent which the minority nationalities occupied in China's whole population in 1982. *China Daily* (16 May 1986: 3) reported that there were then 1.37 million minority cadres, of whom 10,000 held leading posts at county level or above.

Another symptom of the rising representation of the minority nationalities in China's structure of power and influence is the changes required in the management of the autonomous areas under the 1982 Constitution. It is now necessary for the administrative head of an autonomous area to be a citizen of the relevant nationality, so, for instance, the head of the Tibetan Autonomous Region must be a Tibetan. The autonomous governments are also empowered to administer the finances of their areas.

There are of course still strong limitations to autonomy. For instance, Party secretaries of autonomous regions may still be Han. But the policy which the CCP has adopted since the Thirteenth CCP Congress in October and November 1987 is to move towards a greater separation of Party and government authority, the net effect of which is likely to be a reduction of CCP power at most levels of society. Moreover, serious corruption within the CCP has eroded its authority throughout China, with the result that its control has weakened everywhere, including the nationality areas.

From the point of view of power among the nationalities this decline in CCP authority could operate in two ways. The first one is that many officials of the minorities themselves but especially of the Han ignore CCP policy and grab what they can for themselves against the interests both of autonomy and of those they are meant to lead. The second is that more power will go back to the traditional elites within the nationalities and also to the new rising class of entrepreneurs and rich rural peasants or pastoralists. There could in fact be some overlap between these two groups. Though the situation varies from nationality to nationality, the overall trend in the late 1980s appears to be increasing devolution of power away from the centre and towards the nationality areas themselves.

3. TERRITORY and LANGUAGE

One reason why policy towards the minority nationalities is so important, is because they inhabit so vast and sensitive a region. They may constitute only 8 per cent of China's population, but they occupy well over half its area. The five autonomous regions alone account for about five-eighths of PRC territory. Moreover, the nationality lands include most of China's border regions. Indeed, a glance at a nationalities map of China shows that only along the Sino-Korean and northeastern Sino-Soviet boundaries is the population mostly Han.

Some of the minority-inhabited border regions are among the world's strategically most unstable and delicate. One could instance the border with the Mongolian People's Republic, hostile to China from the 1960s to the mid-1980s. It is Mongolians who live along the border, some of whom may wonder why the boundary places them in China rather than Mongolia. The northwestern Sino-Soviet border area is home to the Kazakhs, Kirghiz, Tajiks, Uygurs and Mongolians, of whom the first three nationalities run their own Soviet Socialist Republics on the Soviet side. One of the factors in the drastic deterioration of Sino-Soviet relations in the early 1960s was the flight of thousands of Uygurs and Kazakhs across the border to the Soviet Union in 1962. The Chinese leaders believed the incident to have been engineered by the Soviet Union. At the best of times the presence of people from a single nationality on both sides of an international border will hardly help good relations between the two countries concerned. It becomes worse since the Kazakhs are traditionally nomadic anyway and may be quite happy to dwell at different times on either side of the border.

While it is true that extremely precise delineation of international boundaries is a relatively modern practice, the problem of handling peoples living along its borders is by no means new for China. Already in the second century BC the great Emperor Wudi (140-87 BC) of the Han dynasty (206 BC-220 AD) sent Zhang Qian far to the west in order to contact the Yuezhi people who had been defeated by the Xiongnu. These were a warlike people living in the steppes beyond the Great Wall, and the reason for Zhang Qian's mission was to persuade the Yuezhi to form an alliance with Wudi's court which would relieve pressure on China.

The chapter on history showed that the Chinese fear of invasion was by no means groundless, especially in the north. On several occasions the steppe peoples took over north China, and twice the whole country. Incursions were numerous and sometimes serious. In 763, for instance, the Tibetans occupied the Chinese capital Chang'an for a few days.

It is only fair to add that attacks and invasions were also frequently carried out by the Han Chinese against neighbouring peoples. Thus, Wudi is famous in history not only for the Zhang Qian mission, but for sending armies into what is now Inner Mongolia and Xinjiang. The process of an expanding Chinese territory noted earlier would hardly have been possible if it had always been the Han who suffered rather than initiating the attacks.

Wars have also occurred on numerous occasions through attacks by one of China's neighbouring peoples against another. The Uygur state which helped the Tang against the An Lushan rebellion in the eighth century actually fell in 840 as a result of invasion by the Kirghiz from the north.

Most of the Uygurs reacted by migrating to the west, ending up in their present homeland. The example highlights the importance of migration of nationalities as a factor explaining why particular peoples live where they do. Nomadism has assisted the process of migration and suggests a reason why peoples move about, but war was usually a primary spur all the same. Nationalities or tribes tended to migrate together, and those individuals left behind were absorbed into another community. This explains why a migration led a nationality simply from one 'common territory' to another.

Again the question arises whether such 'common territory' is really part of China. At the time of the migration of the Uygurs from what is now Mongolia, Chinese control over the areas covered by the migration was either non-existent or very tenuous. Strictly speaking, it might not have been in China then. Contemporary Chinese historians adopt a simple solution.

Anything which in the past happened in what is *now* Chinese territory is part of Chinese history, whether or not the land where a particular event took place was ruled by a Chinese government at the relevant time. It follows that the part of the history of the minority nationalities which took place on *present* Chinese territory is also part of China's.

Apart from the migration of the minority nationalities, another type is that of the Han into the minority areas. Naturally it brings people in groups, not in almost entire nationalities or tribes. Although it is certainly not new to the present age, it has gathered momentum since liberation. According to the figures of the 1953 census, only 4.1 per cent of the population of Xinjiang was Han. But by 1982, the Han accounted for 40.4 per cent of all those resident in Xinjiang, having almost caught up to the Uygurs. In 1982 the Han were about three-fifths of the population of the Guangxi Zhuang Autonomous Region, two-thirds of that of the Ningxia Hui and over four-fifths of the Inner Mongolian.

Most of the less populous nationalities live in autonomous areas within provinces. In the southern provinces of Hunan, Guizhou, Guang-dong and Sichuan, there are substantial communities of minorities. The Han province with the largest minority presence is Yunnan, where about one-third of the total population of some 33 million belong to 22 minority nationalities. These include some that are very populous, more than 3 million Yi people scattered widely over the province and more than half China's total Yi population, and over 1 million Bai and Hani, both nationalities more or less exclusive to Yunnan Province. A particularly interesting one is the Thais, whom the Chinese call Dai, but who are culturally and in other ways the same as the Thais of Thailand. There are also· a number of much smaller nationalities, but important in being found in China outside Yunnan only in extremely small numbers. These include the Lahu, Bulang, Jingpo and Naxi.

The PRC region with the slightest Han proportion is Tibet. Even allowing for a substantial military presence, it has the smallest popula-tion of any of China's provinces or autonomous regions, not counting the army about 1.9 million in 1982. Almost all the troops are Han, but less than 5 per cent of the civilians are so, and at least three-quarters of the total population, including the army, are Tibetans. On the other hand, only about half the Tibetans in China reside in Tibet itself and there are also many Tibetans living in India and other places outside China.

Of all China's minority nationalities the Tibetans have the longest and most consistent tradition of self-rule, separate from the Han. There was an independent kingdom in Tibet at least from the sixth century AD. It came under Mongol rule in the thirteenth century, as did China, but by the fourteenth was again semi-independent. The rule of the dalai lamas began in the seventeenth century with the great fifth Dalai Lama (1617-1682) and lasted until the flight of the fourteenth Dalai Lama just after the rebellion of 1959. Nevertheless, Tibet was part of the Manchu Chinese empire and so rule by the dalai lamas did not necessarily mean total independence.

It is very clear that strong secessionist feeling survives in Tibet in the late 1980s, even allowing for the more enlightened policies followed since the early years of the decade. Demonstrations demanding total independence from China flared in Lhasa, the capital of Tibet, in September 1987. The police suppressed the disturbances by arresting many monks who were leading them, and on 1 October violence erupted resulting in the deaths of over a dozen Tibetans. Further such demonstrations occurred during 1988, and during one in December at least one Tibetan monk, and probably more, was killed by the police. The most serious pro-independence disturbances occurred in March 1989, resulting not only in deaths and looting, but also in the imposition of martial law. The Chinese government remains quite determined to preserve the unity of China, which means refusing Tibetan independence. But such incidents can do only harm to the already tense relations between Han and Tibetans.

It is obvious from this account that the minority nationalities' homelands are scattered over the length and breadth of China. In the same way one can expect to find not only different dialects but different languages in the various parts of China. All the minority nationalities have their own languages, except the Hui, who speak and write Chinese, and the Manchus, who once spoke and wrote Manchu but now use Chinese. Some of the nationalities, such as the Mongolians and Yao, have several languages. The main language family is the Sino-Tibetan. Twenty-nine nationalities, accounting for about three-quarters of the minorities' population, speak a language belonging to this family. They live in the central-south and southwest of China and include such peoples as the Zhuang, Dai, Li, Tibetans, Yi and Yao. In addition, seventeen nationalities, mainly in the northeast and northwest, speak Altaic languages, such as Uygur and Mongolian. Several minority nationalities use South Asian languages, including the Va of Yunnan. Finally, there are two which speak Indo-European languages: the minute Russian community in Xinjiang and the Iranian Tajiks in the west of Xinjiang (ZSM: 585-586).

Although almost all nationalities have their own tongues, before liberation only twenty-one used their own written languages. This is not surprising since the literate class is small in all pre-modern societies. Many of those without their own writing simply used Chinese characters. However, some developed significant literatures, especially the Tibetans, Mongolians and Uygurs.

After the PRC was established, the new government encouraged the use of the minorities' languages and in some cases even helped them to devise new writing systems. For instance, the Zhuang people had once developed their own script but it died out and they wrote instead with Chinese characters. In 1955 a new writing system was adopted based on the international phonetic letters, themselves founded on the Latin alphabet.

The Tibetan, Mongolian, Korean and Uygur scripts are still in strong use among the relevant nationalities and show no signs of dying out. In 1960, a new Uygur and Kazakh writing system was adopted based on the international phonetic script. However, though it is still used in some circles, most Uygurs and Kazakhs prefer their traditional written language, which derives from Arabic. Since the early 1980s this has returned to become stronger than ever. Publishing in minority languages was all but suspended during the Cultural Revolution, but has picked up since the late 1970s. As of 1988 it had gathered such momentum that it could legitimately be called an explosion.

The spoken languages of the minorities are likewise strong. Like the written, they suffered difficulties during the Cultural Revolution, for example, broadcasting in some of them was banned. However, such stupidities are now a thing of the past. Nationality areas currently enjoy the services of broadcasting stations using their own languages. Thus, in Inner Mongolia there are two regional stations, one using Mongolian, the other standard Chinese. The only regional television channel telecasts one day a week in Mongolian, the other six in Chinese.

Article 134 of the 1982 Constitution stipulates that 'Citizens of all nationalities have the right to use the spoken and written languages of their own nationalities in court proceedings'. In the primary schools, instruction should take place in the language in common use in the locality, which in nationality areas will often be the tongue of the relevant minority.

On the other hand, the authorities are trying to encourage as many people as possible to understand standard Chinese. Any young urban member of the minority nationalities who aspires to a good job will certainly find it in his or her interests to learn standard Chinese well. This applies also to any Han who is a native speaker of Chinese dialect and so can hardly be interpreted as discrimination against the minority nationalities. The government knows well that successful modernization depends in part on a common means of communication. This can only be Chinese in a country where 92 per cent of the people are Han. However, the authorities cannot discourage the use of nationality languages. So they must urge on minorities knowledge of two languages, especially in the cities. The eventual prospect is for the use of the minority languages to decline. However, I believe sections of the minority nationalities will cling to their own languages, as well they might under official policy, and the radical weakening of Uygur, Tibetan, Zhuang and others is many decades, even centuries, in the future.

4. ECONOMIC LIFE

Although there is great continuity in the practicalities of the territory and languages of the minority nationalities before and after 1949, change is very obvious in their economic life. This term here refers to the economic structure of the societies of the minority nationalities before and after liberation, and the advances in such aspects as industry, agriculture and social welfare which have taken place under the CCP.

Contemporary observers in the PRC, following Marxist categories, divide the minority nationalities of the pre-liberation period into stages of society according to which classes held property and thus power. In ascending order of development these societies are classified as those containing remnants of primitive communism, slave, feudal serf and feudal societies. Another way of categorization is according to how the people produce what they need to live, for instance slash-and-burn horticulturalists, hunters and gatherers, pastoralists or agriculturalists.

Although none of China's minorities lived in primitive communist societies, quite a few maintained some remnant features of such a system. These included the Va, Nu and others of Yunnan province as well as the Oroqens, Ewenkis and Hezhe of the far northeast of China.

According to the 1982 census, there were 23,166 Nu people at that time. In the past they were slash-and-burn farmers, which means that 'every spring they felled trees and let them dry in the sun, burned them to ashes before the sowing, then poked holes in the ground with wooden sticks to sow maize' (Yin 1977: 45-46), but ploughed only a small part of the land with oxen. Classes and a landlord economy had already developed by the middle of this century among the Nu but in some areas private and public ownership of land coexisted; and several households might own and till the soil collectively and share out the crop equally: 'land holdings were not concentrated and the remnants of primitive communism were preserved' (ZSM: 414). It was, however, a poor insecure and backward existence for the wooden tools could never hope to bring about much production.

The Oroqens lived from hunting and fishing, not agriculture. Among them the 'remnants of primitive communism' were shown in the collective hunting groups which formed on an *ad hoc* basis for one season and then disbanded after sharing out the gains equally. The alternative system of hiring horses from horse-owners also existed. In this case the hunter gave part of what he caught to the horse-owner and kept part for his own family.

The example most often cited for the slave society is the agricultural Yi people of Liangshan (literally 'the cool mountains') in Sichuan Province's eastern border regions with Yunnan. There were 5,453,448 Yi people in mid-1982 but only about 20 per cent of them live in the Liangshan region. The first large-scale Yi migration to the Liangshan was in the Tang dynasty (618-907). The slave system in which slave-owners were the dominant class developed in about the sixteenth century and survived until the middle of the twentieth.

The hereditary slave-owning class were called the Black Yi, and made up about 7 per cent of the population. They also owned some 70 per cent of the ploughed land and most of the productive tools. Owned by the Black Yi were three classes of slaves in a descending hierarchy. The highest of the three were the White Yi, who constituted about half the total population. These had to do corvée labour for their owners, and were not allowed to move outside territory under the latters' jurisdiction, but most of the time worked on their own land and could even possess slaves. The next class was about one-third of the whole population. They spent most of their time in unpaid labour for their owners and were subject to sale or purchase at any time. However, even they might be allocated a tiny plot of land for their own use. The lowest of all, about one in ten of the people, could possess no land of their own and simply did the drudgery and dirty work for their owners. PRC sources call them 'talking tools'and record the most frightful tortures to which almost all were subjected for the slightest offence or at the whim of their masters (ZSM: 304-305).

Next in the hierarchy of systems is feudal serfdom. Fei Xiaotong, the PRC's most distinguished ethnologist of the older generation, writes (1981: 45):

> The characteristic of this social system was that peasant serfs were assigned to definite land allot-

ments by their feudal lord under conditions of slavery, and from then on they were bound to the soil for life and remained appendages of the feudal lord from generation to generation to bear the lot of a serf. The feudal lord was free to punish his serfs, take their property, and exact corvée and exorbitant rent in money or in kind according to his will.

Nationalities illustrating this system are the Dai and a portion of the Mongolians.

However, the example of feudal serfdom most often cited is that found among the Tibetans, who were sedentary agriculturalists but also nomadic pastoralists. There were three kinds of landowner in practice: government, religious and private. The great majority of the population were peasants, extremely few of whom owned any land. Some peasants worked land allotted to them by the government, monasteries, lamas or aristocrats. They paid taxes and gave most of the produce to the landowner, but kept some as payment for their labour. Other peasants were simply drafted or hired labourers and worked on land managed by its owners. There was also a group of household slaves, the lowest class in society. These could be bought or sold by the serf-owners.

In the case of Tibet there is a large literature written in defence of old Tibetan society. Dawa Norbu, for example, sees the Tibetan system not only as unique but as one 'in which religion and politics ran parallel without conflict of any kind' (1974: 190). He claims that the peasants were to some extent free because they could 'petition their lord to be relieved from his service' and goes on to say that the answer given depended on such items as 'the plausibility of the petition, the petitioner's influence, and the size of the bribe and his own temperament' (p. 195). But to this writer it is not much defence of a system if, to escape it legally, one required influence and the money to give bribes. Fei Xiaotong does not define precisely what 'conditions of slavery' are. Dawa Norbu claims (p. 192) that the members of his own family had actually preferred to labour on the monastic fields than on their parents' land because the work was lighter. He thus implies a picture quite different from that of downtrodden serfs labouring under conditions of slavery, though it should be added that his parents' possession of land places them above the great majority of peasants.

PRC ethnographers have produced evidence of the most shocking tortures being inflicted on serfs. Exhibitions have been held on the former life of Tibetan serfs, replete with gruesome pictures. On the other hand, Dawa Norbu's picture of law in old Tibet is rather rosy. The 'Thirteen Decrees', believed to have been promulgated in the seventh century AD, were a much milder code than those prevalent in imperial China. While it did include a number of frightful mutilations, such as 'taking out eyeballs', Dawa Norbu states that 'such un-Buddhist punishments' (p. 77) were abolished by the thirteenth Dalai Lama, who died in 1933. On the other hand, the Gelders (1964: 113), who visited Tibet in 1962, claim to have met a Tibetan former serf whose eyes had been gouged out, at the behest of a clerical magistrate, for stealing two sheep from a monastery. 'If we had asked to meet a dozen Tibetans who had been mutilated by their masters we should have been confronted with a dozen', they write. 'But one was enough'.

To reach a fair verdict on old Tibetan society would require a lengthy dissertation and is not my purpose here. However, even Dawa Norbu concedes that Tibet needed reform. He believes it would have happened anyway, without the Chinese (1974: 146-147). We shall never know, though old Tibet's was among the more static of the world's societies. The reality, however, is that it was through Han socialism that reform did eventually take place.

The last major system to mention is the feudal, in which a landlord hired out land to tenant farmers, demanding not only rent but some of the produce, or employed labourers to cultivate his land. In addition to the Han, some 85 per cent of the minority nationality population followed the feudal system in the past, including the Zhuang, Hui, Uygurs, Koreans, Miao and Hani, and most of the Yi and Mongolians. These feudal nationalities were mainly agriculturalists, such as the Zhuang or Uygurs, but included also some pastoralists, like the Mongolians. Among the Hui, Uygurs, Mongolians, Zhuang, Koreans and others, capitalist elements had begun to appear by the time the CCP came to power.

The various nationalities had thus reached extremely different stages of economic development and system when the PRC was established. The CCP was therefore rather careful about the speed with which it implemented socialism. Those nationalities with their own communist movements responded quickly. In this category one could single out the Koreans and the Mongolians, both of whom had been thickly involved in the War against Japan, or the Uygurs who had come under Soviet influence in the 1930s. In Yanbian, Jilin, where the largest Korean community lives, the land reform movement already began in July 1946; while among the Mongolians it lasted from 1947 to 1952. The Uygur peasant areas began land reform in September 1951, concluding it at the end of 1953. Some nationalities comparatively well integrated with the Han undertook land reform soon after liberation, an example being the Zhuang which completed the process in 1953.

On the other hand, some nationality areas took a little longer to uproot the old property systems. The Liangshan Mountains Autonomous Yi Prefecture was set up in October 1952 and orders issued banning the torture of slaves. It was not until these proved unsuccessful that the CCP launched the democratic reform movement which lasted from 1956 to 1958 and completely eradicated the system of slave ownership and emancipated the slaves. In Tibet the old system remained more or less intact until the rebellion of March 1959. In April the National People's Congress in Beijing ordered democratic reform, including land reform, the abolition of the serf system, the appropriation of the monastic estates, and the suppression of the lamas' political power.

The government was likewise slower in setting up people's communes among some of the minority nationalities than the Han. Although the establishment of people's communes dates from 1958 among the Han and such minority nationalities as the Uygurs, Koreans, Miao and Mongolians, it was not until 1965 that the process began, and 1975 that it was completed, among the Tibetans. The Yi of Liangshan, the Nu and Dai set up communes in the late 1960s and one portion of the Yao in 1970. However, in the early 1980s the commune system has been progressively dismantled everywhere in China, not only among the Han but the minority nationalities as well. What has replaced it is the production responsibility system, by which families, groups or individuals sign contracts with the village management for particular tasks. In effect, family farming or pasturing has revived, but it is unlikely that large-scale monastic estates will return, let alone serfdom or slave-owning.

It is probably in part as a result of the overthrow of the past oppressive economic system that the years since 1949 have seen substantial economic growth in the minority nationality areas. To set this statement within a relevant context it is worth noting that the population of the minorities grew at an annual rate of 1.11 per cent between the 1953 and 1964 censuses, as against a faster 1.59 per cent per year for the Han over the same period. But between the 1964 and 1982 censuses the minorities reversed the trend of the earlier decade and grew in population rather more quickly than the Han, annually 2.94 per cent as against 2.04 per cent. Over the whole period 1953 and 1982, the minority population rose by 90.4 per cent, that of the Han 71.2 per cent (Zhang 1984: 22-23).

Since food is the basic necessity of life and the minorities are overwhelmingly rural anyway, we begin with the economy of the countryside. Whereas the minority population nearly doubled between 1952 and 1982, grain production in 1984 rose by 260.1 per cent and the overall value of agriculture was some four times what it had been in 1952. The sheep population more than doubled, the pig multiplied by more than thirty times. In other words, if we start from a base year which had already seen the Chinese economy, and especially that of the minorities, on the road to recovery, then the grain levels have somewhat kept ahead of the population, but not drastically, while improvements in other areas of rural development have been rather more impressive.

At the time of liberation industry was, not surprisingly, far more backward than agriculture or pasture among the minority nationalities and urbanization had made little progress. While there were the beginnings of a working class among the Manchus, Koreans, Zhuang, Hui, Bai and others, most had virtually none or none at all. In 1985 the total value of industrial output in the autonomous regions was thirty-eight times what it had been in 1952. Production of such vital commodities as coal, oil, electricity, iron and steel, and cloth had all risen enormously. (Based

on figures in ZTN: 81). Much of this industry is located in what have become Han areas of the minority regions, such as southern Inner Mongolia. Moreover, it is Han people who have taken the initiative in developing industry and still manage most of it. Minority areas supply most of the raw materials. Nevertheless, it is unquestionable that people from the minority nationalities have learned an enormous amount about industrial development in the last thirty years or so, and are benefiting greatly from it through the development of electricity, machinery and so on.

One factor enabling industry to develop in the minority nationality areas is an improved communications system. In 1985 there were 12,495 kms of railways in the autonomous areas, as against 3,787 in 1952, while the advance in road building was even greater with 254,100 kms in 1985 but only 25,900 in 1952. While the communications system in China's nationality areas is still very backward when compared against that found in a developed country - many of the roads are extremely rough and badly maintained - it is incomparably better than it used to be.

The last aspect of economic development to mention is social services. Medicine is of course not new to the CCP period. Many nationalities had quite highly developed traditional medicines, for example the Tibetans and the Uygurs. These have been maintained under the CCP. The extent of medical services available to the masses has increased enormously. In 1952 there were 17,000 'hygiene technical personnel', including doctors and nurses, but in 1985 the number was 423,700, about twenty-four times as great. In Tibet and some minority nationality areas of Yunnan medical service is free for everybody, which is not the case in most of China. The level of the services may be extremely low in many places, but it is at least available to all. As a result incidences of serious disease and premature death have shrunk greatly. Pre-liberation infant mortality rates among the minority nationalities were over 20 per cent but have now fallen drastically; in the Yanbian Korean Autonomous Prefecture, admittedly among the most advanced of the minority nationality areas, it is claimed as being on a par with the highly developed countries.

For economic development education is a particularly crucial factor. The following statistics from the Statistical Yearbook of 1986 (ZTN:

82) tell a familiar story of overall growth.

Numbers of Students among China's Minority Nationalities
(in thousands)

	1952	1965	1978	1983	1985
Tertiary college	2.9	21.9	36	59.6	94.1
Secondary school	92	390.7	2,526.2	1,911.8	2,448.7
Primary school	1,474.2	4,350.0	7,685.6	8,129.0	9,548.1

The CCP encourages education among the minority nationalities also by injecting special funds into the development of schools and, at tertiary level, by lowering the standards demanded for admission for minority students, as compared with Han.

However, serious problems remain. It is disturbing to find the enrolments in secondary schools actually fall between 1978 and 1983. According to Li (1983: 18) the proportion of minority students to the total relevant population is still below the national average, except among the Mongolians and the Koreans. This means that illiteracy will be somewhat slower to disappear among the minority nationalities than the Han. Boys get preference in the educational system over girls, so that equality between the sexes becomes an even more distant social objective. There are still inequities between boys and girls in Han schools, but they are even more serious in the minority areas.

Over the years since liberation the government has invested an enormous amount of money in helping economic development in the nationality areas. In 1982, 98 per cent of Tibet's budget took the form of central government subsidies. Tibet is still among the poorest areas of China, but was once even poorer. Despite persistent shortcomings it is beyond doubt that the standard of living has risen enormously among China's minority nationalities since the accession of the CCP to power. In terms of availability of consumer goods, housing and variety of food, levels have accelerated since 1978. The improvement is particularly noticeable in the countryside and can be largely attributed to the introduction of the production responsibility system.

5. RELIGION

Among the most important aspects of culture of China's minority nationalities, for many *the single* most significant, is religion. Among the fifty-five minorities there is an enormous diversity of religions. The strongest is undoubtedly Islam, which prevails among the Hui people and most of the Xinjiang nationalities, such as Uygurs, Kazakhs, Kirghiz, Tajiks, Tartars and Uzbecks. Another still very strong religion is lama Buddhism, to which the Tibetans and Mongolians adhere. Hinayana Buddhism is still followed, especially among some of the nationalities of Yunnan like the Dai and Bulang. Various forms of polytheism or nature worship are traditional among the Hani, Miao, Yao, Va and others, while shamanism still exists among the Ewenkis, Daurs and Oroqens of China's far northeast, the Xibo in northwest Xinjiang, and in Yunnan. Christian missionaries converted portions of the Yi, Miao and others in western Yunnan, and some of the Russians and Ewenkis still adhere to the Eastern Orthodox Church.

These religions gained enormous influence over virtually all aspects of the people's lives. More or less all the popular festivals were based in some way or other on religion. Islam affects the marriage practices, clothing and diet. Moslems regard pigs as unsacred and dirty so they do not eat pork. They have very specific death rites. They circumcise their sons. Islam also affected the status of women among its adherents in China, for instance by allowing four wives for each man, by forcing women to wear the veil, and by excluding them from various forms of public life. Lama Buddhism attracted or forced very large numbers of males into the clergy, who held an extremely high social status. Among the Mongolians, at the height of lama Buddhism's influence, some quarter of all able-bodied men were connected with the church, while in Tibet in the middle of this century, about one-fifth of the entire population belonged to the clerical order.

The last example shows the economic impact as well. So many people in the monasteries could not fail to exercise a bearing on production. The monasteries occupied much of the best land and also absorbed a high proportion of the people's income. According to Han sources, the impact of lama Buddhism was one of the main reasons why the population of Tibet sank from some 2,000,000 in the 1730s to about

1,200,000 in 1951 (Wang 1984: 44-55).

The economic influence of the clergy gave them enormous political power. Tibet is the most obvious example. The dalai lamas were not only religious but also political leaders and made Tibet into a theocratic state. Although other minority nationalities did not base their politics on theocracy, religion was most certainly used to buttress political rule. It was part of Islamic doctrine to demand political power and the idea of the holy war against the infidel has been a root cause of anti-Chinese uprisings in the past.

The religious differences between the Han and minorities hardly contributed to good inter-nationality feelings in old China. This was especially the case with Islam. One contemporary scholar has written (Israeli 1980: 47):

> The Muslim Chinese felt that they belonged to an alien people and regarded themselves as superior to their neighbours. Just as Chinese hatred towards Muslims may be traced back to the Yuan, when Muslim bureaucrats were the masters, so the Muslims may have preserved their feelings of superiority since those days, and reinforced them by their communal distinctiveness and by their claim to be the adepts of the Word of Allah and the disciples of His Messenger...
>
> Muslim counter-contempt for the Chinese was so deep-seated that when a Chinese became converted to Islam, it was customary in many parts of China to have him eat crude soda to obtain internal purification.

When the CCP came to power it determined to overthrow the economic and political power of the religious bodies, both Han and minority nationality. It also tried to prevent any religions from disrupting the unity of the nationalities. As for the social influence, its policy was that any religious tenet which directly opposed the social change which the CCP was advocating should be suppressed, but that anybody was free to believe in and practise any religion.

This policy obviously included atheism. Chinese spokesmen consistently argue that the traditional societies of the minority nationalities allowed no religious freedom. Thus, Fei Xiaotong (1981: 29-30) claims that 'Certain religions were imposed on some minorities under reactionary rule. They enjoyed no religious freedom. They were not free to be atheists or to believe in some other religion.'

In accordance with their policy, the Communists progressively took over the monastic lands and destroyed the political power of the clerics. In all nationality areas some religious buildings were taken over for other purposes, such as schools or museums, but others were left to house clergy or for the worship of the people.

The social side of religion posed the biggest problems for the Communists. There were of course many questions with quite straightforward answers. The human sacrifices of the Va were part of their nature worship, which was no reason for not banning them. The same logic stopped Muslim polygamy and the forcing of boys into lamaist or other monasteries. On the other side of the coin, there was no conceivable reason for forbidding Moslems to abstain from pork. Other problems were not so simple. Should Islamic women continue to wear the veil? The answer was that the practice was degrading to women and should go. Should women be allowed to worship along with men in mosques? This was left to the nationalities themselves to decide. In practice very few women do so, although the gender segregation inherent in the ruling is arguably also degrading to women. Should the religious schools found among so many nationalities in the past continue to operate? Here the answer was no, for while the CCP was prepared to tolerate religions it saw no reason why it should allow their propagation.

This limited religious freedom changed to outright persecution during the Cultural Revolution. Mosques, temples, lamaseries and churches were closed down in more or less all parts of China, including nationality areas. The lamas, imams and other clergy were sent into production or at any rate expelled from their religious abodes. Han Red Guards went into the minority regions and actively tried to prevent belief in or practice of any religions. The grounds were that all religion represented feudalism. It was part of the machinery of exploiting classes to oppress the masses, and should be suppressed. The emphasis on class struggle as the key link prevented any exemptions for minority nationalities.

Some of the actions of the Cultural Revolution's zealots reached an extent of barbarity which is still a source of great bitterness to the minority nationalities. In Tibet and elsewhere many monasteries were destroyed. A particularly famous example is the dGa'-ldan Monastery, some 60 kms outside Lhasa, once the central temple of the dominant Yellow Sect of lama Buddhism. When in 1985 I visited this magnificent and ancient monastery, where the first dalai lama and Yellow Sect founder Tsong-kha-pa (1357-1419) is buried, I learned from a senior monk that Red Guards and their supporters had demolished it during the Cultural Revolution. Though it has since been partly restored, the still visible evidence of destruction shows shameful thoroughness on their part.

It comes as no surprise that the policy and practice of the Cultural Revolution caused bitter resentments among religious devotees. With the fall of the gang of four in October 1976 the door was opened to change back to the former policies. Religion revived strongly all over China. It is currently stronger among many minority nationalities than in the 1950s and shows no signs of weakening. Chinese social scientists ascribe this strength to reaction against the persecution suffered during the Cultural Revolution. They admit, however, that religion will be influential among the minority nationalities for a long time to come (Wang Guodong, 1982: 77-78).

Among the Mongolians, lama Buddhism is still practised among the rural masses, who are pastoralists. The Tibetans, also lama Buddhists, are probably the most devout of all China's nationalities. A young anti-Han Tibetan I met during a visit to Tibet in 1985 estimated religious believers at 100 per cent of the Tibetan population. A Han government official who had lived in Tibet sixteen years and with whom I chanced to share a hotel room, gave it at 90 per cent, 'apart from government workers and party members'. I suspect the former estimate is closer to the truth than the latter.

In central Lhasa's great Jo-khang Temple, founded by the famous King Srong-bstan sgam-po (d. 650), numerous people of all ages, both male and female, stand in long queues to make votary offerings of rancid yak butter lamps to the Buddha. Some Tibetans, especially but by no means only older women, prostrate themselves in front of the Jo-khang Temple or in stages proceeding through the nearby central market of Lhasa. Everywhere, there are numerous older people, mainly women, revolving prayer-wheels. In the countryside, almost all the houses have prayer flags fluttering from the roof.

In Xinjiang the number of functioning mosques stood at about 14,000 in 1982, many of them new. The number of Moslems to visit Mecca from Xinjiang in 1983 was over 300, the highest for one year in all Xinjiang's history; all went at their own expense. One imam told me that he propagates Islam with a loudspeaker. As far as I know there are still no Islamic schools permitted, although some probably operate unofficially and without government permission, and seminaries have certainly revived. Although I did not see any women in the veil, I was told that some still wear it in parts of Xinjiang. One writer claims (Kheir, 1984: 277) that 'the custom of circumcision has almost disappeared among all Chinese Muslims'. On the other hand, Sauvageot and Donzé (1980: 150) write that circumcision, though suppressed during the Cultural Revolution, has come back since, 'but the government has encouraged the practice of this operation in hospital arguing that it is a medical act', rather than a religious one.

Among the Dai people of Xishuang banna in Yunnan, every village includes a temple, often newly built. Many young males still spend their adolescence as 'little monks', receiving instruction in the sutras. For the overwhelming majority of people, Buddhism remains a vital part of life.

Although the CCP is currently prepared to tolerate religions among the minority nationalities, it remains true that social pressures against them are strong, especially in the cities. Lessons in the schools are hostile to them. The way up the social scale is through Marxist materialism, not religion. Although there have been press complaints about CCP members among the minority nationalities attending religious celebrations, the fact is that a Party member is forbidden to believe in religion. CCP membership remains a sign of high social status all over China, including in the minority areas.

In Tibet, the number of functioning temples and monasteries is far lower than it used to be. Before 1950 there were several thousand but there are now only about 200. I visited the five in and near Lhasa and, although all had their devotees and pilgrims, only the Jo-khang was always crowded. I rarely saw a young person with a prayer-wheel. The very young who are currently in the Han-influenced schools, are likely to grow up less devout than their elders, even though national pride will keep most of them believers in Tibetan Buddhism.

While there are young novices in the monasteries, the great majority of monks are old or very old, and very few are middle-aged because of the break during the Cultural Revolution. The senior lama at the dGa'-ldan Monastery told me that there had once been 3,300 monks in residence there, but in 1985 only 200. At the 'Bras-spungs Monastery near Lhasa, once the largest of the Yellow Sect temples, I learned that there had been 7,700 monks before 1950, but in 1985 the number was only 300. Chinese sources claim that many were forced into monasteries in the past against their will (e.g. Peng and Yang 1983: 86). It is well known that each family was expected to give at least one son to the religious life, so there could be at least some truth in the allegation. On the other hand, the suppression of religion in the 1950s, 1960s and 1970s included the forcible *prevention* of people from entering the clerical order, and a momentum, once broken, does not fully re-establish itself easily.

One minority nationality where religion appears very weak is the Koreans. During a visit to Yanbian in 1986 I neither saw nor, despite enquiry, heard of a single functioning Buddhist temple. Although a Christian Church was planned for Yanbian's capital Yanji, the Koreans show but little interest in reviving their own traditional religion.

The economic power of religion is now broken, but the political is far from dead, though much weaker than in the past. The demonstrations for Tibetan independence which occurred in 1987, 1988 and 1989, were led by lamas and monks who continue to enjoy great influence among the ordinary people. Many Tibetans still worship the exiled Dalai Lama, and no visitor to a Tibetan area can escape numerous requests for his picture. In a lama temple in Hohhot in Inner Mongolia I saw his image publicly displayed for reverence. For a Uygur or Kazakh, adherence to Islam is often still a sign of loyalty to his or her own nationality in contradistinction to the dominant Han. Religion remains an obstacle to 'the unity of the nationalities' sought by the CCP. Yet it is my impression that Israeli's comments quoted earlier and referring to the past are simply not applicable to the present. Han-minority antagonisms based on religion survive, and at least in Tibet strongly, but they are not as poisonous as they used to be, either during the Cultural Revolution or before liberation.

6. COURTSHIP and MARRIAGE

An aspect of culture much influenced by religion is marriage practices. Just as there is a wide range of religious beliefs among China's minority nationalities, so their marriage customs show a great variety and have received some attention from Chinese ethnographers, especially in recent years.

A few general observations may be made. On the whole married partners of the great majority of nationalities in China tend strongly to come from the same class, and mixed marriages, where husband and wife belong to a different nationality, are rare. Sauvageot and Donzé (1980: 97) comment that Tibetan women are deeply religious and thus hardly ever marry 'other than religiously', which excludes Han husbands. 'Marriages between Tibetan men and Chinese women are even rarer', they write. But one can extrapolate more broadly from this particular example to mixed marriages in general. They may be more common now than they used to be, but in fact that says very little.

In the past, and today, the great majority of families among ordinary people were nuclear, that is husband, wife and offspring. Most nationalities, including the Han, practised polygamy in the past, but only among the rich.

The great majority of nationalities, especially those which follow Islam, are male dominated in their marriage and family customs, though the situation is changing gradually as modernization progresses. Patriarchy is overwhelmingly common. The exception is the Naxi nationality of Yunnan and Sichuan provinces. There are several types of family among this people, including the matriarchal in which genealogy is reckoned along the maternal line from a common ancestress, inheritance is matrilineal and the family head is often female (Yan 1982: 64).

All nationalities have their own festival days. Most of these involve large-scale gatherings one of the functions of which is courtship. A good example is the Nadam Festival of the Mongolians, held in the summer. It features 'breathtaking horseraces and wrestling, admirable archery, resolutely fought chessboard arts, and enchanting songs and dances' (ZSM: 73). At the other end of China, Guangxi in the south, the Mulam people hold hillside fairs every year after the autumn harvest or around the spring festival. Their main entertainment is cockfighting, but there are also lion dances and singing, and a chance for young people to meet members of the opposite sex.

The minority nationalities vary greatly in the freedom young people enjoy, before marriage, in their relations with members of the opposite sex, and in the choice of their spouses. On the whole, the nationalities of the south and southwest are very much less prudish in these respects than the Han.

An example is the Va people. 'Young men and women meet in groups in one place where they sing love songs to each other and make presents of betel palm and tobacco to show affection; and then may live together' (ibid.: 360). The Miao are another of the many southwestern nationalities for whom premarital sexual relations were - and to a large extent remain - part of the procedure for finding a mate. An old painting from the Qing dynasty (reproduced in Ito 1978: 244) shows young Miao couples dancing round a pole. Part of the accompanying commentary reads, 'On the day after the beginning of spring they place a wooden pole in the open country and call it an ancestral spirits' pole. On it they hang a white flag. The men and women exchange belts....and make love'. The meaning of the exchange of belts is that the girl could refuse an advance from a man by failing to reciprocate his offer of a belt.

Yet the liberality implied in these popular customs is not total by any means. In the case of the Va, the parents need to consent before a couple can actually marry. The man's family sends his bride money, but if the woman's parents do not agree to the match they will prevail on their daughter to come home. Among the Miao, and many other nationalities, a matchmaker arranges the actual marriage, which requires the agreement of the bridal couple's parents.

A recent traveller among the Miao (Wong 1984: 326-327) describes how formerly a chicken had to be killed in front of the parties concerned before a marriage could be approved.

> After the chicken was cooked whole, the size of both its eyes was examined. If the eyes were identical, it symbolized a happy union. But if they were of different size, it was considered a bad omen and the wedding plans automatically were cancelled.

Fortunately such superstitions have weakened recently. It is still the case, however, that on the wedding day a Miao bridal couple may not converse publicly or sleep together. In the following period, the wife lives some of the time with her husband's family, but mostly with her parents. It is not until the first child is born that she takes up permanent residence with her husband.

The courtship customs of the Juno of Yunnan were very similar to those of the Miao, but the actual marriage did not take place until after the first child was born. Although there was much freedom before marriage it became one-sided afterwards. The man 'was still allowed to have contact with other women' whereas 'women had to maintain strict chastity' and 'usually abstained from social activities' (Wang Jun 1982: 92). Divorce and separation were both rare.

In traditional times, the rule among many of the nationalities was that the onus for finding a mate lay with the parents. It was the families that arranged the marriage, not the couple themselves. Nationalities in this category included the Han, the Koreans, the Mulams mentioned above, and all the Islamic peoples. Families usually engaged the services of the inevitable matchmaker. Among the Islamic Sala people of Qinghai province there used to be the couplet:

> If there are no clouds in heaven above
>> it will not rain,
> If there are no matchmakers in the world below
>> there will be no marriages.

Among the Salas too, and indeed other Islamic nationalities, divorce was extremely easy for a man. He needed only to tell his wife 'I no longer want you' and she would be forced to leave his house. On the other hand, she enjoyed no reciprocal rights.

Conditions have improved greatly for Islamic women recently in China. Nowadays, in the cities the choice of partner is usually made by the young people themselves, though parents retain the right of veto. Kheir (1984: 274-275) reports that among the Hui, Uygur, Kazakhs and other Islamic nationalities young people who fall in love 'usually inform their parents of their intention of marrying and obtain their approval without difficulty'. He adds that, at least among the Kazakhs, the man's family sends a matchmaker over to the potential bride's to make sure she is a suitable wife for him, by 'carefully examining her behaviour, physical appearance, and her conduct while serving guests at home'. If the matchmaker reports favourably, the future bridegroom's father calls on the woman's family and sorts out a date with them for the wedding. This is a grand occasion and, among all Islamic nationalities, still usually involves not only the state but the local imam who performs the Moslem ritual. The merry-making which follows the ceremony includes much song and dance, and a great deal of food, but no pork or alcohol, which are strictly forbidden.

The marriage practices of the Tibetans are worth special note since, like so much else about that nationality, they include features more or less unique in China. In the past the man's family took the initiative in choosing a bride. The method was to cast a horoscope to establish if a woman was suited and, if she was, to gain agreement from her family and set an appropriate day through the aid of an astrologer. Social contact between unmarried young men and women was rather free, but after marriage the female was subordinate even if, as often happened, her husband had come to join her family rather than the other way about. Divorce, remarriage, either of men or women, and the bearing of children out of wedlock were all comparatively acceptable socially.

In old Tibet estates were held as a family unit through one male who served in the government as an official. Consequently it was the practice among the nobility for the brothers of an official to share his wife. If a noble family produced no sons, then it might adopt a male who would serve as an official and thus hold the estate. He would marry all the daughters. If any of them wished to marry somebody else, she must forfeit all claim in the estate. As a result of these economic factors both polyandry and polygamy became widespread among noble and then propertied and other rich classes.

Among the poor the nuclear family was the practice. Serfs required their owner's permission to marry and could be forbidden for their whole life. Usually marriage among serfs took place within a single estate; but an owner could buy a partner from another estate for one of his own serfs, or carry out an exchange by sending back another in lieu of money.

The collapse of the old Tibetan class system after 1959 has resulted in the drastic weakening of most of the customs outlined. However, the influence of lama Buddhism is still strong and it has helped maintain some remnants of polyandry because of the interconnection between economic and religious factors.

The CCP has attempted to bring about equality between the sexes in China, not only in Tibet but all the other nationalities as well. The achievements and failures have been mixed in the implementation of that policy, but even a minimum of success must bear upon marriage practices. Those directly hostile to gender equality have been suppressed, such as concubinage and the inequitable divorce customs especially among Moslems. During the Cultural Revolution, the CCP tried to stamp out the courtship gatherings found among so many of the nationalities of Yunnan, Guangxi and elsewhere, but failed. These occur again now, including the premarital sexual intercourse they involve.

7. LITERATURE

There are two broad categories of traditional literature among the minority nationalities. These are formal literature and long narrative or epic poems. The former category includes religious tracts, histories, or poetry, and is written down. Consequently, it is associated with, and overwhelmingly written by and for male members of the rich and educated classes. The latter category tends strongly to be popular literature, it is almost always oral and handed down from master to disciple being but rarely, if ever, written down.

Written Literature

Clearly formal literature is confined to those nationalities with written scripts, and the five which have produced most extensively are the Tibetans, Mongolians, Manchus, Uygurs, and Koreans. More or less all Korean formal literature was created outside what are now the borders of China, so the following discussion leaves the Koreans aside.

The present Tibetan script came into use in the seventh century. Apart from translation of foreign religious works, the Tibetan educated classes also produced annals and chronicles, written legends, liturgical works, poetry and magical or prognosticative tracts. An enormous amount of such pre-eleventh-century Tibetan literature has been discovered in the caves of Dunhuang in Gansu province. The central feature of medieval Tibetan literature was that it was more or less entirely religious. Lamas such as Rong-ston sMra-ba'i Seng-ge (1347-1449) wrote enormous numbers of exegetical and philosophical works, though that did not exclude general topics like logic and poetics.

The Mongolians have been lama Buddhists since the sixteenth century, so it is natural to find a strong Tibetan influence in their literature with many Mongolian lamas learning Tibetan. Mongolian literature excels in religious and historical tracts. Among the historical texts are those by the scholarly lama Lobsangdanjin of the seventeenth and eighteenth centuries, worth mentioning here because he lived in the religious centres of Inner Mongolia and Shanxi, both in China. The Mongolians have a deep and spontaneous sense of poetry, which features alliteration and rhyme occurring on the first words of a line, not the last.

'Virtually all Mongolian literature is characterized by a nomadic and hunting background and imagery' (Jagchid and Hyer 1979: 216-217) so that it closely reflects the society which produced it.

The most important branch of early Manchu literature is historical. A few archives survive from the early seventeenth century, that is to say from before the time the Manchu Qing dynasty conquered China (1644). For most of the Qing period the court edicts, historical records and some others were written in both Chinese and Manchu. After the conquest, under the influence of great Manchu emperors such as Kangxi (1662-1722) and Qianlong (1736-1795), the Manchus adopted the forms of Han Chinese literature. It is noteworthy that the eighteenth-century novelist Cao Xueqin was a Manchu. As the conceiver and author of a large part of *Honglou meng* (*A Dream of Red Mansions*), which can lay as good a claim as any to be China's greatest novel, he holds a vitally important place in the literature of China's nationalities. Yet Manchu literature became so fused into Chinese during the Qing dynasty that it can only with difficulty be distinguished, and often not at all.

On the other hand, Uygur formal literature shows very little Chinese influence. Surviving pre-Islamic Uygur literature is also more or less entirely religious in nature, including Manichean or Buddhist prayers or tracts. The first great secular work is the long poem *Kutatku bilig* (*Happiness and Wisdom*), completed in 1069 by Yusup Has Hajip. It is an allegorical, not narrative, work which 'is concerned with the duties of the ruler toward the ruled, the qualifications for the various classes of officials and an evaluation of a number of moral precepts' (Lattimore 1975: 242). Although Yusup Has Hajip did establish a tradition of long poems, later Uygur literature was almost entirely oral until our own century.

Oral Literature, Long Narrative Poems

This brings us to that other category of minority literature, the long narrative poem. Long narrative poems are found among most of the minority nationalities, although this is a genre singularly lacking in Han Chinese literature.

We begin with China's 'three great epics': The Tibetan *Gesar*, Mongolian *Jangghar*, and *Manas* from the Kirghiz nationality (1982 population: 113,999), a Turkic people who live in western Xinjiang just north of the Tajiks.

Gesar enjoys two very special characteristics. The first is that it is one of the very few works in all Tibetan literature down to the present century the theme of which can be described as secular, even though there are religious elements. The other is that it has the reputation of being the world's longest epic. A contemporary Chinese encyclopedia (Zhang and others 1983: 89) claims that an old Tibetan artist 'took up two years in reciting and singing ten sections of it, altogether 4.2 million words, and the saying went that there were still twenty-one sections he had not recited'.

Gesar is a magic hero, the son of a god who is reincarnated into the family of a small tribal chief and rises to be king. According to Snellgrove and Richardson (1968: 177-178), medieval wandering bards 'sang the glories of ancient mythical kings, identified with the great kings of the four quarters, known conventionally as China, India, Persia, and the North'. Gling was a small kingdom in northeast Tibet from the fourteenth century on, and its royal family became identified with the King of the North; 'vast accumulations of legendary and popular religious material became associated with this epic hero', Gesar of Gling. The tale tells of his exploits and wars against rivals, evil goblins and other enemies.

There are many versions of the epic of Gesar and theories on its origin. It remains to this day a popular evolving oral tradition. It is found all over Tibet and in all Tibetan communities, being especially popular nowadays in the region of Changdu in eastern Tibet. The epic also spread to Mongolia along with Tibetan cultural influence.

Jangghar Khan is a legendary hero among the Mongolians of northern Xinjiang, called the Oirad or Kalmuck Mongolians. Like so much else relating to traditional literature, the epic was all but lost during the Cultural Revolution but in 1979 a special committee was set up in Xinjiang to find some of the numerous versions and thus revive it. One singer was found deep in the mountains who knew ten chapters of the epic by heart. As of mid-1984, over one hundred different texts from sixty-five works on Jangghar Khan had been found. One Mongolian researcher has found evidence of an old pastoralist of the late sixteenth or early seventeenth century living in what is now Xinjiang who knew no less than seventy works about Jangghar. When his khan heard him perform, the monarch gave him seventy pieces of gold and a title. The story shows that the origin of the epic can be dated at least to the sixteenth century, and probably much earlier since there were numerous versions even then. It suggests northern Xinjiang as the original home of the epic, since the Oirads had lived there from the fifteenth century. Later the epic spread to many other places, including Russia and other Mongolian people (Ren and Qi 1984: 34-35).

The content of the epic revolves around Jangghar Khan's defence of his homeland against an evil demon. Interwoven into this theme and the wars it necessitates are love stories, marriages, law suits, quarrels among warriors and so on. Jangghar's enemies are characterized as demons.

The epic *Manas* records several decades of the Kirghiz nationality's Manas family and its central theme is national struggle against the nearby Oirad Mongolians, the very people who had spawned Jangghar as a legendary defender of their own homeland. There are many other themes interspersed into the struggle and Lattimore, basing himself on Soviet sources, writes (1975: 258) that 'many of the Turkic national tales, legends, and heroic episodes have been amalgamated by the Kirghiz' into this huge national epos which is *Manas*. It also shows details of Kirghiz society 'with descriptions of battles, family life, marriage, death ceremonies, feasts'. Like other epics it has developed and evolved from oral traditions over the centuries, and remains very popular indeed among the Kirghiz both in the Soviet Union and China. No wonder that a Chinese compendium of the nationalities sums it up by saying that 'this great work of 200,000 lines is an encyclopedia of the Kirghiz nationality in ancient times' (ZSM: 216).

Living just east of the Kirghiz are the Uygurs, the most populous of Xinjiang's nationalities. The oral literature of the Uygurs falls into several genres, and some, such as proverbs, are in no sense either epic or narrative. However, there are also extended heroic fairy tales like that of the hero who fights a seven-headed monster. Another genre is Uygur

47

popular tales. Many of these belong to general Turkic and Iranian Inner Asian story cycles and derive from written folk stories from other parts of Inner Asia (Lattimore 1975: 247). There is also a long tradition of romantic tales. Nowadays the Uygurs speak of their 'twelve famous love stories' of which the best known is that about Erip's love for the princess Senem and the difficulties the couple faces. Unlike many Uygur love stories, *Erip and Senem* has a happy ending.

Long Uygur narrative poems can be sung by themselves. But they also make up part of the Uygur form known as the *mukam*. There are three sections of a *mukam*, termed 'classical songs', narrative songs', and 'song and dance'. The first is a male solo prologue and the third well explained by its name. It is in the second section that the singer tells his story through a long poem. The *Twelve Mukams* are the most famous of Uygur performing arts compositions and a source of great pride to the nationality which produced them. They are of unequal length but last about twenty hours if performed immediately one after the other.

At the other end of China from the Uygurs, geographically speaking, are those many minority nationalities of southern China, in regions like Yunnan, Guangxi and Guizhou, and it is to them that we now turn.

There is a certain consistency in thematic patterns running across the narrative long poems of the nationalities in southern China. One contemporary Han scholar has identified three stages in the content of long poems dealing with the early history of the nationality (Li 1984: 6-8). The first is the 'fairy tale on the creation of the world'. The content here deals only with the creation of the world and of humankind, which in fact means the particular nationality to which the individual poem belongs. Among the Yao people is a long poem about a goddess who makes the sky, then the earth, and finally people. Everything in the poem is mythical and there is no treatment of any event which could hold historical veracity.

The second stage is the poem which deals not only with the creation of the world and of people, but also their development, such as how humankind first used fire or entered early peasant society, or cultivated the family or the arts. 'This kind of primitivistic narrative poem bursts through the limitations of the fairy tale in its content, and includes such matters as ancient traditions and direct records about ancient life and customs'. Nationalities with such poems include the Zhuang, Miao, Hani, Jingpo and Lisu. Among the Yi people of Liangshan and the Yao there are examples which even recount wars of ancient times.

The third type is poems about migration explaining how a particular nationality got to its present territory. These are special in that they 'have almost completely thrown off the domination of mythical thought', but on the contrary record reality 'and have obviously been formed and developed on the basis of ancient traditions'. Nationalities such as the Zhuang, Yi and Hani have produced long narrative poems of this kind.

The most developed is the heroic epic. A few have been rediscovered in recent years for the southern nationalities, including several among the Dai and a version of the Gesar epic among a Tibetan community in Yunnan. But it appears that the heroic epic does not occupy in the oral literature of the southern nationalities the vital place so evident among the Mongolians, Tibetans or Turkic peoples of Xinjiang.

The last topic to mention is the universal one of love. In today's China the most famous specific example is *Ashima* produced by the Sani branch of the Yi nationality. It concerns the beautiful Ashima abducted into a forced marriage with the local rich man's son. Her brother rescues her from this fate but she is accidentally drowned as they return home after the victory. The Sani identify with the positive characters in the poem, which has become a creator of images of good, evil, loyalty and courage in their society.

There is thus a sociopolitical aspect to the long narrative poems. Each one establishes and strengthens an identity for the nationality which has produced it. The poems tell of the origin of the nationality or how it got to the place where it rightfully belongs. They relate the great deeds of the national heroes, and the defence of the homeland against other minority nationalities or the Han. They are an excellent source of a nationality's pride in its own existence and characteristics. In this way they constitute intensely political statements.

8. MUSIC, SONG and DANCE

'I n the treasury of China's arts, those of her minority nationalities are a resplendent component' (Yin 1977: 94). PRC evaluations of the arts of one or a group of Chinese minorities use a phrase such as this so regularly as to suggest that it is seen as a truism, a slogan. Yet, like many other truisms, it is perfectly valid and its being a slogan does not detract from the sincerity of those who use it.

Some of the high points of Chinese art were in fact produced by people from the minority nationalities. Two examples which leap to mind are the magnificent Potala Palace in Lhasa, completed under the Fifth Dalai Lama (1617-1682), and the amazing Buddhist sculptures of the Yungang Caves near Datong in Shanxi province, the earliest of which date from the fifth century. To my mind, these are wonders not only of Chinese but of world art.

Each branch of the arts of China's nationalities is worthy of a complete study in itself. It is necessary to be highly selective in a survey such as this. I have chosen to confine this treatment to the performing arts, and more specifically to song and dance and the closely related topic of musical instruments. The performing arts follow directly from the discussion on literature, since the epic poems, being created not to be read but chanted to an audience are themselves a branch of the performing arts. There is a strong tendency among China's minority nationalities for the performing arts to be more tightly blended into the folk society than the more elite forms like painting or architecture. Of all the performing arts, song and dance, including music, are the most important and widespread branch among the minority nationalities. Another reason for selecting song and dance for inclusion in the survey is that there is less readily available material in European languages on this topic than on other equally important art-forms such as architecture, painting and sculpture.

The art form which combines song and dance dates back in China centuries before the time of Christ. Today's nationalities integrate the pair in many different ways. In the first place, they perform songs and dances in one programme and assume that a single troupe should be able to include items of either form in the same evening. But it is perhaps more important that among many of the minorities, the same artists both sing and dance as part of the same item. One could instance the Kazakhs and Uygurs. The popular, humorous duets of the Uygurs show a man and woman singing and dancing as part of their courtship, the music and action getting more and more vigorous and leading to an excited climax.

Song and Dance Themes and Content

Given this integration of song and dance, it is natural to find that both forms cover very similar or even identical themes. The true folk arts are closely based on the actual livelihood of the people; whereas song expresses their everyday emotions in words, dance does so in movement, and music adds to the emotion and artistry of both.

In virtually all cultures dance is one of the main methods men and women use to woo each other, so courtship is a major theme of dance among the nationalities. Among the Dong people of Hunan, Guizhou and Guangxi, the Reedpipe Dance is a collective mass dance in which people 'walk and dance and at the same time accompany themselves on the reedpipe' (Baoerhan and others 1986: 100-101), and the same could be said of the Yi, the Hani and quite a few other nationalities of southwestern China. The traditional custom among the Miao, whose courtship was discussed in Chapter 6, was 'to choose a level piece of ground in the first month of the year' where 'the men blew reedpipes while the women shook bells, and they sang and danced around and around'. The Reedpipe Dance remains popular today as a collective dance among the Miao, but the women are most likely to be empty-handed, not to shake bells (Wang 1980: 86). It is also performed by professional troupes as a refined item which expresses love between the sexes, even if it is, in this form, clearly too contrived to fulfil a specific courtship function.

Love is traditionally the most popular of all themes for folksongs. It is true that the Red Guards of the Cultural Revolution tried to suppress the love songs of the minorities as reactionary, but this absurdity has vanished even more thoroughly than the influence of the gang of four, with the result that love songs are as popular today as ever. The following is the lyric of a typical Kazakh folksong (ZMX: 251-252).

Her name is Red Wheat,
She and I are inseparable,
I sent her treasured gifts,
Gold inlaid belt and whip.

Her name is Red Wheat,
On days I do not see her,
How anxious I feel,
Beautiful Red Wheat,
My love for her is unswerving.
I think of her day and night.

Another of the myriad ways by which a man can express his love for a woman appears in the well-known Mongolian folksong on the beautiful Hanmixiang (Dong 1981: 27-28).

What shakes the mountain peaks
Is the four hooves of the black horse;
What locks my heart
Is the two eyes of Hanmixiang.

The pinetree branches beneath the sun's rays
Are inseparable from their shadow;
Hanmixiang and I
Shall love each other all our lives.

The red sandalwood tree beneath the moon
Is inseparable from its shade;
Beautiful Hanmixiang
Can never leave my heart.

Apart from their charm, these lyrics show the symbolic power of the horse in Kazakh and Mongolian society, the first by its reference to a whip as a treasured gift, the second to the trembling caused by hooves. The horse dominates nomadic peoples like the Kazakhs and Mongolians and innumerable folksongs sing the praises of this strong, mobile and beautiful animal.

Imitation of the horse and its rider forms one of the major bases of Mongolian dance movements. Xu Shuying, a leading PRC dance educator, writes that the Mongolians' 'swaying gait exaggerates their expertise in riding horses' while the 'bent forward stance and shaking of the shoulders', which occur so often in Mongolian dance, 'depicts riding on the backs of galloping horses'. She suggests also other movements of living creatures which find their way into dance. The Mongolians see geese and eagles as symbolic of heroism so the 'powerful movements of the arms' in their dances 'represent the virile, indefatigable geese'. The Dai people revere the peacock, regarding it as an omen of happiness and good fortune. The Peacock Dance is a famous traditional item imitating the peacock's movements, including the way the bird drinks, preens and struts, and remains a favourite with contemporary professional companies and their audiences (*China Daily*, 24 September 1982: 5).

Returning to the world of human beings from that of the fauna which shares the life and territory of the minority nationalities, we find that both song and dance express the work and all kinds of everyday activities of the people. Labour chants are among the most numerous of short folksongs among those peoples whose work can benefit from the synchronization of movement which rhythmic song assists. It lifts the spirits and helps feelings of comradeship to sing as one labours. The Miao 'Song of the Lumberjacks' illustrates the point. One or two leaders alternate with a chorus which sings 'au iye' after each line (He and others 1959: 106).

> The wood is large,
> Very large.
> Lifting wood is like an insect crawling.
> This log is big,
> We're moving it quickly,
> We're taking it down,
> To build a big house.

Dance also expresses labour. The content of the Dong nationality's folk dance Celebrating a Bumper Harvest is shown in its title; the dancers play reedpipes to express their joy and excitement at a prosperous season and plentiful food. Dances of this sort have come to make up, in reformed versions, a substantial proportion of the repertory of the professional companies of the PRC. The Hourglass Drum Dance of the Yao nationality was traditionally performed only on the first and fifteenth days of the first lunar month to sacrifice to one of the Yao gods, but has become a popular collective dance for festival days. In its professionalized form it is danced by one or several couples, each man holding an hourglass drum with one hand and beating it with the other during the dance. The dance movements express celebration over a good harvest, tilling the land, building a house, making an hourglass drum, and other such actions connected with labour and production.

The traditional function of the Yao people's Hourglass Drum Dance as part of a sacrifice to a god leads to the important topic of religion. The dance also provides a good example to show how song and dance might provide part of a ritual for a religious occasion, even if the content is only partly religious. On the other hand, the traditional societies of the minority nationalities were all strongly religious, so it is natural to find their secular songs and dances shot through with allusions to religious practices, ceremonies and ideas. The vigorous shaking of long handkerchiefs in Mongolian dance is said to have derived from exorcising fever spirits from sick people through this action.

It is the lamaist Buddhist nationalities, the Tibetans and Mongolians, who provide the best examples of fully religious dance. The Tibetan *'cham* is part of a long religious ritual held in a temple. It is in no sense entertainment but a ritual for driving out spiritual and human enemies. The performers put on awesome masks and thus impersonate the various divinities. 'Each movement and gesture of the dance, which is accompanied by the music of long trumpets, shawms, drums and cymbals, follows a strictly ordained symbolism' (Snellgrove and Richardson 1968: 246). The accompaniment also includes chanting, so that this can claim to be a real song-and-dance form. In Hohhot, Inner Mongolia, I visited in 1982 a lamaserie where the masks for a very similar religious dance form, as well as long trumpets and other musical instruments, were prominently displayed. I learned that the twenty or so lamas of the temple still perform the dance three times a year with the aim of driving away evil spirits. In Tibet, the *'cham* dance survives but is no longer common. A lama I met at the 'Bras-spungs Monastery denied there were any monk-dancers there but claimed there were some at the temples of Shigatse. At the Sera Monastery outside Lhasa, the masks are carefully preserved, but apparently rarely if ever used.

Religious dances are based upon the beliefs of a particular nationality and thus emphasize its identity. But a more widespread type of content with the same effect is those songs and dances about the history and heroes of the nationality. In Chapter 7, there was discussion of narrative or epic poetry on the histories of the various peoples. Short folksongs about Gesar or a host of other heroes are also very common among the nationalities.

Large-scale dances on national heroic exploits have a long history and remain in vogue today. In 1275 the court of Khubilai Khan, the Mongolian who unified China under his nationality's rule in 1279, commissioned a special military ritual dance which reviewed the exploits and military conquests of earlier Mongol rulers from the time of the great Chinggis Khan earlier in the thirteenth century (Jagchid and Hyer 1979: 240-241). Also traditional but recently rearranged is the Yi people's folk dance Leaping Palace, which concerns a big battle fought successfully by one branch of the Yi in Yunnan against the oppression and cruelties inflicted by the soldiers of the ailing Chinese Tang dynasty (618-907) toward the end of its rule. There are three sections in the dance: 'Going to Battle', 'The Battle', and 'Triumphant Return'. The leaping palace is the strip of ground with a clump of bamboo where the Yi soldiers lay in wait for the Tang soldiers before defeating them. The site resembles a palace, hence the dance's name. The main accompanying instrument is the reedpipe. The dance traditionally occupies three days from the morning till sunset. Many minor items and subplots are woven into the overall work, including the Reedpipe Dance.

The revolution of contemporary times has given a different slant to most of these songs and dances but generally encouraged or allowed their preservation. It has also led to a whole category of songs and dances on topics of direct political relevance for the contemporary revolutionary age, propagating the values and policies of the CCP. Political propaganda is of course not new. In 1275 a dance-epic in praise of the Mongol conquest was undoubtedly political propaganda within the context of its own time. But since the CCP and Chinese socialism derive only from the present century, their particular type of political propaganda can certainly be called new.

The folk arts are never completely static. So there is no reason why a people should not create folksongs and dances based on the styles of the old society but espousing the values of the new. This is what has happened among the minority nationalities. Some revolutionary songs and dances follow the tunes or dance-movements of old more or less unchanged, others devise new tunes or motions in the style of the old. The extent of change tends to depend upon the degree of professionalization - the closer to authentic mass folk art, the less the reform.

There is much in the content of traditional song and dance that could be described as revolutionary, such as labour and the struggle of the poor against the oppression of the rich. Themes that are new include reverence of CCP leaders and praise for its policies, especially the 'unity of the nationalities'. Songs with trite and direct propaganda are fortunately much less frequent now in the PRC than they used to be, and should not obscure the possibility that the people of the nationalities may well wish to propagate the same messages as the CCP, such as raising the standard of living of the people. Yet it is true that the new revolutionary songs and dances on contemporary themes experience a much more rapid turnover than the traditional items. They inevitably lack the permanence of the more genuinely authentic and spontaneous folksongs and dances handed down from the past.

Musical Instruments

Song and dance needs no musical instruments to accompany it. The first can be perfectly adequate musical accompaniment to the second. The Oroqens of northeast Inner Mongolia have but few instruments and 'because the simple and plain dance movements cannot fully express their inner thoughts and feelings, quite a few dances are accompanied by song' (Qiu 1981: 81). Yet among most minorities some instrumental accompaniment is normal. Sometimes only a drum, gong or percussion is used, or a combination of the relevant nationality's instruments. Naturally, the closer song and dance comes to authentic folk art, the less refined and complex it is likely to be. But among most nationalities, ability to play musical instruments properly is widespread or universal, and not restricted just to a few special people. So there is no reason why a real folk performance should not include extensive instrument accompaniment for song and dance.

Space permits discussion of only a few from the vast range of existing minority instruments, and of course only those used to accompany song and dance. They include examples of stringed, wind and percussion categories and from a range of nationalities.

A particularly significant stringed instrument is the horse-head fiddle of the Mongolians. The name of this kind of fiddle derives from the image of a horse's head which is nowadays invariably found at the end of the stem to add Mongolian flavour. There are two strings, tuned a fourth apart, which are played with a bow. The performer places the instrument, with the stem pointing upwards, between his legs or, if sitting cross-legged on the ground, just beside him, and bows across the strings, not between them as is done with Han two-stringed fiddles.

The soundbox is made of pinewood and covered with horse or sheep hide. However, its most distinctive feature is its shape, which is trapezoid. The sound of the horse-head fiddle is fairly low in pitch and volume. It has a characteristic *glissando* and is especially suitable for accompanying soft and delicate lyrical tunes.

An interesting example of a plucked stringed instrument is the *ravap*, popular among the Uygurs and Tajiks of Xinjiang. It dates from about the fourteenth century. There are five strings, and of them the pair on one side of the centre is tuned to the same pitch, as are the two on the other, so that only three notes can be sounded from the open strings. The point of this device is to enable the very rapid repetition of a single note, which is a principal feature of *ravap* music. The instrument is used both solo or in ensembles and to accompany song and dance performances. Its soundbox is hemispherical and there are two wings protruding from the stem, giving the *ravap* an unmistakable appearance. During performance the player holds the instrument high across the chest just below the shoulder.

Wind instruments of various kinds are found extensively among the minorities. These include flutes and a wide variety of reed instruments. Among the Han, one of the most ancient of all instruments is a mouth organ called *sheng*. It consists of a series of pipes pointing upwards and placed on a circular base at the side of which is an aperture where the player blows or sucks. Similar in their performance principle is a wide range of reed-pipes and calabash mouth organs popular among the southwestern nationalities.

The former are made up of a number of reed pipes fitting into a thin shallow wooden cylinder into which the player blows to produce the sound. This instrument is found among the Miao, Yao, Dong and other nationalities. The Miao instruments nowadays usually have six reeds, the larger ones reaching as high as four or five metres from the stem, or as low as eight or nine inches. Even among one nationality reed-pipes vary enormously in size, tone and structure. Across nationalities the differences are greater still.

The calabash mouth organ is popular with the Yi, Dai, Nu, Naxi and other nationalities. The reeds vary greatly in number and fit into a base shaped like a calabash. There is a pipe leading into the 'calabash' and it is through this that the player blows to produce the sounds. As with the reed-pipe, the structure, tone, and range may vary widely from one calabash mouth organ to another, even within the same nationality.

Both reed-pipes and calabash mouth organs are very ancient indeed, dating back to the Western Han dynasty (206 BC-9 AD). In a tomb in Yunnan province from that period, a bronze calabash mouth organ and a pottery figurine with the instrument protruding from its mouth have been unearthed. There are also literary references, one of them showing cultural high-handedness on the part of the Chinese court. In 995, so the standard history of the Song dynasty (960-1279) informs us, a delegation came from the southwestern 'barbarian tribes' (*Man*) offering products of their region as tribute. The reigning Emperor Taizong (976-997) summoned them for audience, and 'commanded them to perform song and dance of their own country. One person played the calabash mouth organ (*piaosheng*), the sound of which was like a mosquito or a gnat' (Songshi: chap. 496, 3859b).

The Chinese of those days were not interested in finding beauty in foreign instruments. Fortunately they are today more appreciative of the musics of their own country's minority nationalities. A major compendium of minority instruments typically describes the sound of the calabash mouth organs as 'bright, clear and melodious' for those of the high range, 'mellow and mild' for those of the medium range, and of the lower as 'vigorous and deep' (Yuan, Mao and others 1986: 124), all generally quite complimentary.

No account of the instruments accompanying the songs and dances of China's minority nationalities can overlook the large array of drums. These are the key to providing rhythm.

The most ancient of these percussion instruments is the bronze drum which dates back well over 2,000 years. Over 500 ancient bronze drums have been unearthed in Guangxi alone. They are found among the Zhuang, Miao, Yi and other nationalities of Guangxi, Guizhou, Yunnan, Sichuan, Guangdong and Hunan. Originally they were used for military or ritual purposes or as a symbol of political power but are now mainly used to accompany dance. As its name implies, it is made of bronze, including the face, which carries characteristic designs. The drum is placed on, or hung from, a stand and beaten with a stick.

Among the Dai is the 'elephant leg drum', so called because of its shape. Again one side only is beaten, but with the hands not a stick. The drum is hung with rope from the shoulder.

Several nationalities have drums shaped like an hourglass. The Yao version is long and narrow and can be held in the centre with the left hand and struck with the right. The most famous is the Korean hourglass drum which is somewhat fatter and heavier. It is suspended from the shoulders in front of the player, whose left hand hits one face gently while the right strikes the other with a small bamboo stick.

A much smaller instrument is the circular *dap*, or Uygur hand-drum, with one face only. It is held between the knees or above the shoulders and hit with the fingers. Metal rings around the frame give the hand-drum a characteristic high-pitched sound. This drum is very ancient, examples being depicted on the walls of the caves in Kuqa, which date from the third to the ninth centuries AD.

Since liberation, it has been consistent government policy, even during the Cultural Revolution, to inherit and preserve the traditional instruments of the nationalities. In most periods, especially since 1978, the minorities have even tried to revive the use of obsolete instruments. However, along with preservation has gone reform. As part of the professionalization of the arts, more and more folk instruments are manufactured in factories, rather than by hand. The strings of instruments are made of nylon or metal, rather than horsehair or silk. The new reed-pipes tend to be larger and more complex than their ancestors. Reforms of these sorts have inevitably affected the tonality of the instruments to some extent.

The Social Context of Song and Dance

Among all the minority nationalities, song and dance and musical performances have always been woven into the social life of the people. A contemporary account says the following about the Koreans (ZSM: 47):

> The rich and varied song and dance arts are loved not only by young men and women but even white-haired old people, who constantly sing and dance. Whenever there's a festival they always gather together and sing and dance to their heart's content. During rest-time in the fields or work-place, if one person takes the lead in singing or beating the hourglass drum, people will stamp in rhythm, sing or begin dancing gracefully. Sometimes during glad family events, they dance and sing happily, making an entertaining 'family song and dance party'. Old ladies in their seventies or children of five and six all sing and dance enthusiastically.

These comments could apply to past or present or to a wide range of nationalities. The 'glad family events' include weddings, birthdays and others. Mongolians, Uygurs, Kazakhs and many others have for centuries regarded song and dance as a family as well as communal affair.

Family or very small-scale performances of song and dance could be indoor affairs, but any occasion involving the masses was open-air because buildings large enough for so many people were very few, and those that might exist were either not open to the common people or only for worship. Song and dance at the Nadam summer festival of the Mongolians or the great gatherings of the Uygurs were held in a square or similar open place, and the same was so of the performances which formed part of the courtship gatherings or the harvest or other festivals of many of the nationalities.

We enter here on two main reasons why the people of China's minority nationalities attended performances, either as participants or spectators: courtship and religion. Both provided not only themes for songs and dances but also occasions for performing them. The courtship function of festivals throughout China already emerged in Chapter 6.

The connection of song and dance with religious observances is strong in virtually all the nationalities. Among the Yao people, steles attest to 'beating the hourglass drum' as part of religious rituals since ancient times. Sacrifices to ancestral gods were important regular rituals, and involved 'beating the hourglass drum to celebrate a bumper harvest'. In at least one Yao community in southern Hunan, officials in the dynastic past 'would arrange for local Yao nationality men and women to stamp their feet in time to song, dance and the beating of the hourglass drum, in order to assist in the music of the sacrificial ritual' in honour of particular gods (Yaozu 1983: 111).

This example shows mass participation in song and dance performed for a religious purpose. Even in an Islamic nationality such as the Uygurs similar practices still prevail. The mass Sama dance is still performed by hundreds of male Uygurs in some city squares outside the mosque on festival days such as the Islamic New Year, Corban.

Examples of more formal religious items, that is those in which the masses do not take part as performers, are also easy to find among the minority nationalities. The Tibetan and Mongolian 'cham dances are clearly religious, not only in content but in their place and occasion of performance.

Although there is great continuity with the past in contemporary China, there are also radical changes in the performing arts. The main one springs from the process of professionalization, which in China derives from Han socialism.

The CCP government has set up professional companies to perform the songs and dances of the nationalities. The main one performing the arts of peoples all over China is the Central Nationalities Song and Dance Company, established on 1 September 1952 in Beijing, but there are numerous others, mostly catering for one or a few nationalities only. These professional companies began by seeking the services of 'old artists' and giving them full-time jobs. In this way the companies could help maintain, as well as reform, the traditional arts of the various nationalities.

The CCP authorities have also established formal art schools in all the relevant areas of China to train the next generation of artists. They include the Arts School of Inner Mongolia, set up in 1957, of Xinjiang, in 1958, and of the Tibetan Autonomous Region, in 1980. Old artists helped in the training from the beginning, but there was substantial contribution also from the Han because the new regime insisted that a general education, including Marxism-Leninism, was essential for performers. Illiteracy, ignorance and feudal thinking should all be wiped out. In the 1980s, the trend is towards handing over as much as possible of the control and teaching in these schools to the members of the relevant nationalities themselves.

Professional companies can and do perform in the open air. But they tend to prefer formal theatres where they can perform all the year round protected against the extremities of rain, cold or wind. To cater for their needs, many theatres have been built. The overwhelming majority are in the urban regions, where the professional companies themselves are based.

9. CONCLUSION

In considering its attitude towards its minority nationalities, the first problem any state faces is to decide on the precise extent of its territory. Only thus can it know precisely who comes under its jurisdiction. The PRC government has declared its territorial claims and did so at the beginning of its rule. Many people outside China and in Tibet itself consider Tibet to have a legitimate claim to independence, though the PRC has consistently denied it. But even if one excepts Tibet, China still faces a gigantic problem and responsibility over how to treat its minorities. Nobody would now deny that Guangxi, Sichuan or Yunnan are legitimately integral parts of China, and very few would even challenge the PRC's claim to Xinjiang, where the Han have exercised influence and power even longer than the Uygurs.

Having established its territorial limits China faces a range of options on how to treat the people living within its borders. If the Han treatment and attitude towards the minority nationalities is viewed historically, then it becomes clear that the PRC is the first Chinese government to work out a comprehensive and coherent policy towards the nationalities.

The emperors were usually prepared to encourage or allow extremely discriminatory assimilative processes to take place, or simply do nothing unless it affected government revenue. Chiang Kaishek's regime was also high-handed and thoughtless as far as the minority nationalities were concerned. Its own Ministry of Information stated officially (China Handbook: 245) that its 'border' secondary education gave special emphasis 'to a clear understanding of the Chinese race and nation', suggesting that the common attitudes which contributed to national unity should be seen at least in part in racial terms, as if the minorities existed merely to benefit the Han.

The CCP may have been uneven in the implementation of its policies, but it is at least aware of the problems. It has taken more effort to think through its policies creatively than any previous government. Although great Han chauvinism survives strongly at the grass roots level, the CCP has made a greater attempt to oppose and suppress it than have previous political orders. One would need to except the years of the Cultural Revolution from this generalization, but even that would leave the CCP in a much better light than earlier regimes. The CCP has during most periods characterized its policy towards the minority nationalities as autonomy within a multinational unitary state, in other words somewhere between pluralism and assimilation, but a long way from either.

The essence of the CCP's policy of autonomy is to work towards leaving as much administration and power as possible to the minority nationalities themselves, so long as they recognize that they are part of a socialist China. This approach leaves many aspects of the nationalities' livelihood unchanged. It encourages the minorities to use and develop their own languages and to retain many of their old customs, courtship and marriage practices. It allows continued adherence to their religions. However, it has not permitted the indefinite persistence of systems which are oppressive to the masses or discriminate against women, such as slavery, serfdom and polygamy. Moreover, it has overthrown classes it considers exploited the masses. This means that while monasteries, lamas, mosques and imams still exist and practise their religion, they may not own estates or wield political power.

In economic terms the policy of autonomy implies strong attempts to raise the standard of living of the minorities. This is mainly carried out by the Han in the first instance, but as time goes on should be transferred more and more to the minorities themselves for implementation. There is no reason at all why a Tibetan, Va or Yi should not understand industry as well as a Han, even though it has been slower to come to these three cultures. Universal literacy and education, a long and healthy life are just as beneficial and desirable to a Mongolian, Nu or Korean as to a Han. However, it is important to note that the modernization process which brings higher standards of living also implies greater integration of the minorities' economy into that of China as a whole. The result will probably be the long-term weakening of those cultural and other aspects which distinguish the minority nationalities from the Han.

It is arguable that the Han ought not to interfere at all, but rather follow a policy of benign neglect. That would at least allow the minorities to develop exactly as their own rulers please. But it would also leave the minorities much more backward than the Han, it would allow the most ferocious systems of exploitation of the past to remain in operation, and ignore shocking inequalities. It would thus be more discriminatory and paternalistic than the present policy.

In the field of the arts there has been over history substantial influence both of the Han over the minority nationalities and vice versa. Nobody would challenge the desirability of mutual influences in the arts. But a one-way deluge from a dominant people drowning the cultures of less powerful and populous nationalities is a very different matter. There is no doubt that the Chinese of the past looked down on foreign civilizations and were unconcerned if those in or near its borders suffered extinction. Contemporary policy, however, is that mutual influences must be consistent with the preservation of the styles and 'democratic' elements of the contents of minority nationality arts, in other words not assimilative.

Arts which preserve national styles foster a sense of national identity. Both past and present governments have been willing to various extents to tolerate a feeling of identity on the part of the minorities. However, separateness from China is a different matter. When the arts became a vehicle not only for national identity but for inciting secession, then Chinese governments of all periods, including the present, have wished to suppress them, whether they did so or not depending on opportunity or power rather than wish. The fact is that the arts in general, but especially the performing arts, can influence a people deeply, because they set up images of good and evil which bring strong influences to bear on national attitudes. Folk songs and dances shape the minds of people without their knowing it, and hence reinforce the common culture which is one of the hallmarks of a nationality.

So how far in fact has the PRC allowed autonomy to the songs and dances of its nationalities? These arts survive on two quite different levels. The genuine folk arts are stronger than ever in the 1980s, but there are also many professional troupes. So while attempts to allow autonomy have been broadly sincere and successful, on the non-folk level professionalization and modernization have tended to strengthen Han influence and to whittle away the differences between the various cultures.

Professionalization means that the training of the future members

65

of the full-time companies becomes a function of the Han-dominated state which not only chooses who will enter the performing profession but ensures their education in Han-interpreted socialist ideology. It raises the standards of living and the social status of performers, and the level of their arts. It clearly affects the content of those arts because it adds a socialist strand which is more or less uniform throughout China and is not part of the original folk arts.

Ironically, professionalization has brought another influence, other than Han, which is external to the minority nationalities, namely that from the West. The First Asian Dance Symposium held in Beijing in the fall of 1982 expressed serious misgivings about the impact of Western practices and arts on the national dances of Asia. One visitor, after seeing a performance by one of China's best song-and-dance troupes, told Xu Shuying of his surprise and shock at finding that the 'choreography was very Western and jazzified' (*China Daily*, 29 September 1982: 5). This kind of Western influence extends not only to dance but is beginning to affect virtually every aspect of economics, society and culture, and even politics.

The second half of the twentieth century is an age of excellent and improving communications. These go everywhere together with modernization and the expertise which derives from professionalization. As China modernizes, its communications system will improve rapidly. Cross-influence among nationalities will grow in all fields, political, cultural and economic, because everybody will know more about what others are doing. Since the Han are 92 per cent of the population, their influence is bound to dominate.

This process does not mean the end of the traditional manners, aspects of society or arts of the minority nationalities. It does mean that they are changing in ways to a large extent dictated by Han socialism. The implication is that reality in the nationality areas of China is farther from pluralism along the pluralism-assimilation spectrum than policy. The widespread corruption of CCP and government officials, whether Han or minority, is likely to make them more arrogant towards the people they lead than CCP or government policy would allow, and less willing to implement genuine autonomy. The major demonstrations in

Tibet since September 1987 in favour of independence have produced the opposite effect there from the one intended: less autonomy, not more.

In many countries modernization has swamped and is destroying the cultures of powerless minorities. In China, for all the corruption and imperfections in the implementation of policy, there is a conscious attempt at the highest and some other levels to allow political and economic autonomy to the minority nationalities, and to preserve many of their customs, performing arts forms and styles, and other aspects of culture. This may mean that, seen in worldwide terms, China's record on its minority nationalities in the face of modernization becomes a comparatively good one.

PORTRAITS OF

CHINA

EIGHTIETH BIRTHDAY (Han)

THE WEAVER (Li)

EXPRESSION OF STRENGTH (Yi)

SILHOUETTE (Yi)

THE RED HAT (Ewenki)

74

A STAR (Dong)

HEART OF THE DRAGON (Hani)

SOCIAL WORKER (Dulong)

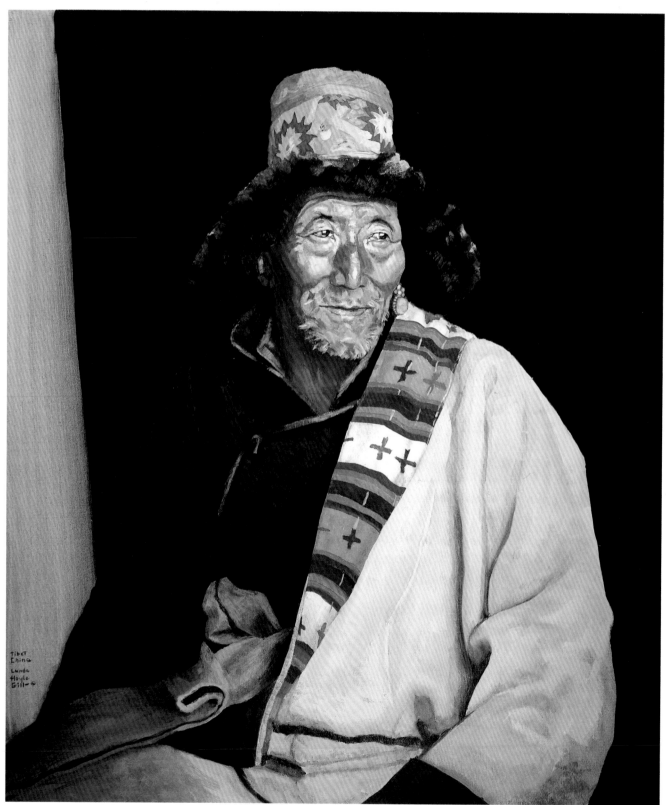

TRADITIONALIST (Tibetan)

78

TURQUOISE GIRL (Tibetan)

Jing
China

Lunda
Hoyle
Gill—
©

BEAUTY (Jing)

80

BABY (Han)

81

STRAW HAT (Han)

FATHER AND SON (Miao)

MAN AND YURT (Mongolian)

SILVER AND BEADS (Xibo)

FLAMES (Yi)

RED SILK (Va)

BRIGHT RIBBONS (Tu)

DANCING HANDS (Qiang)

PINK TURBAN (Lahu)

90

SILK AND SILVER (Miao)

I LOVE NATURE (Daur)

INNOCENCE (She)

93

BEADS AND STRENGTH (Lisu)

MOUNTAIN MAN (Gaoshan)

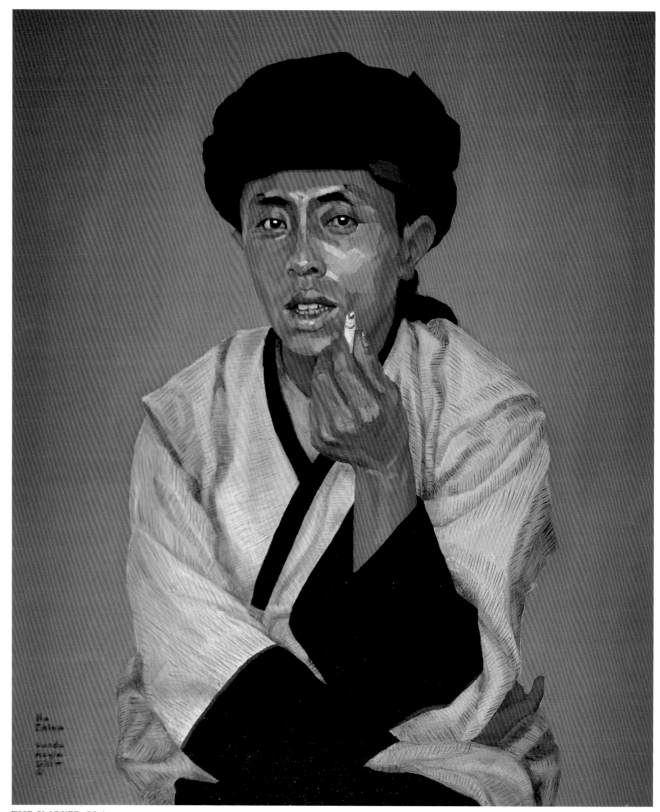

THE SMOKER (Nu)

CORN GROWER (Bouyei)

FESTIVE DRESS (Naxi)

PEACOCK DANCER (Dai)

BRIDE IN PINK (Mongolian)

Jingpo—
China—
Lunda
Hoyle
Gill—P.R.S.A.
©

PROFILE OF STRENGTH (Jingpo)

FARMER'S DAUGHTER (Miao)

MOTHER AND CHILD (Miao)

103

BRIDE IN RED (Han)

A LEADER (Pumi)

105

WOMAN WITH WHITE KERCHIEF (Uygur)

106

OLD BEARDED MAN (Uygur)

YOUNG STUDENT (Dongxiang)

108

WHITE AND BLUE (Hui)

EYES OF CHARACTER (Yao)

110

COLORS (Korean)

FEATHERS (Kazakh)

ENJOYING A PEACH (Bai)

113

MUSICIAN (Tajik)

114

MUSICIAN (Uygur)

115

WOMAN AND DOOR (Tibetan)

ACTOR (Tibetan)

117

CHILD ACROBATS (Han)

MONK (Tibetan)

119

FABRIC TREASURES (Manchu)

JEWEL (Yi)

THE NATIONALITIES

ACHANG: population - 20,400, distribution - Yunnan. Related to the Jingpo they live as mountain farmers in the extreme west of Yunnan on the Burma border. They have a colourful culture, and their religion involves belief in primitive spirits and ancestor worship.

BAI: population - 1,131,100, distribution - Yunnan, in the high plains east of Burma where they are rice-growers. Their ancestors were among the rulers of the Nanzhao kingdom, which lasted some 250 years until 902. Its successor kingdom the Dali was conquered by the Mongols in 1253, and since then Bai territory has been part of China. They have retained close ties with the Han for centuries and are among the most acculturated of all China's minority nationalities.

BAOAN: population - 9,000, distribution - Gansu. A small group speaking a Mongol language living in a defined pocket near the Qinghai border. They are Islamic and in many ways culturally close to the Hui.

BENGLONG: population - 12,300, distribution - Yunnan. They live in three defined pockets in the southwest, close to Burma. Speaking a Mon-Khmer language, related to Va, they are subsistence farmers, having cultural traits very similar to their Burmese neighbours. Some of them follow a form of Hinayana Buddhism.

BOUYEI: population - 2,120,500, distribution - Guizhou, but only in the south, close to Guangxi, where they share a way of life not unlike that of the Miao. They practise polytheism and ancestor worship.

BULANG: population - 58,500, distribution - Yunnan. Distinct from their neighbouring minority peoples, they speak a Mon-Khmer language and have a closely-related culture to those of Burma and Laos. They are good farmers with an economy based on shifting cultivation. Some of the people can speak Thai, Va or Chinese.

DAI: population - 839,800, distribution - Yunnan, in the far south near the Burma border. They have a close affinity with the people of Thailand. They are Hinayana Buddhists, their villages include temples and their festivals, among which the most famous is the "splashing water festival", reflect their religion. Their arts include rich and colourful dancing and singing.

DAUR: population - 94,000, distribution - Inner Mongolia, Heilongjiang and Xinjiang. Having a tradition of grain and vegetable farming and animal husbandry, in the far north of the country, they now also rely on logging, hunting and fishing, and have an affinity with the Mongolians.

DONG: population - 1,425,100, distribution - Guizhou, Hunan and Guangxi, in the small border area where all three provinces meet. Speaking a Thai language, they have a close affiliation with their southern neighbours. Currently their economy is based mainly on agriculture and forestry. Their architecture features covered bridges and multi-storeyed drum towers.

DONGXIANG: population - 279,400, distribution - Gansu, Xinjiang. They have close ties with the Mongolians, but are Islamic by religion.

DULONG: population - 4,700, distribution - Yunnan. As farmers, the Dulong have their villages in mountainous far northwest areas on the Burma and Tibet borders. They speak a Tibeto-Burman language very similar to Nu. Their traditional religion is nature-worship, with belief in spirits.

EWENKI: population - 19,300, distribution - Inner Mongolia and Heilongjiang. A Tungus people, speaking a Tungus language, their traditional religions include animal and ancestor worship and shamanism, as well as lama Buddhism. Once migrant hunters of China's far northeast, these people, over the last thirty years, have given up their birch-bark and hide tents for a more settled life. However, they still hunt, breed deer, tend flocks and farm.

GAOSHAN: population - 380,000, distribution - Taiwan and Fujian. Gaoshan are the aboriginal mountain people of Taiwan. They are millet farmers, hunters and until the early 1900s were headhunters. They speak a Malayo-Polynesian language and may originally have migrated from the Malay Archipelago.

GELAO: population - 53,800, distribution - Western Guizhou, Guangxi and Yunnan.Surrounded by many other small pockets of minority groups in the southwest, the Gelao live in three small distinct areas as mountain subsistence farmers and hunters. Although there is a Gelao language, only about 6,000 people still use it, the other members of the nationality speaking Chinese, Miao, Yi or Buyi languages.

HANI: population - 1,058,800, distribu-

tion - Yunnan. Speaking a Tibetan-Burmese language, they live in the south along the Vietnam, Laos and Burma borders as subsistence farmers. They practise polytheism and ancestor worship.

HEZHE: population - 1,500, distribution - Heilongjiang. Neighbouring the Soviet Union in the country's far northeast, these Tungus-Manchu speakers are, in terms of population, China's smallest minority nationality. As farmers, they concentrate on rice-growing. Their traditional religion is nature-worship and shamanism. Their main form of art is sung folk narrative.

HUI: population - 7,219,400, distribution - Ningxia, Gansu, Henan, Hebei, Qinghai, Shandong, Yunnan, Xinjiang, Beijing and Tianjin. The chief distinguishing feature of the Hui is that they are Muslims. They are widely dispersed in many occupations, in particular as restaurant owners and butchers. Apart from the adherence to Islam, their culture is basically the same as that of the Han, and they speak and write Chinese.

JING: population - 12,000, distribution - Guangxi. A small group of coast-dwellers who live in the south, neighbouring Vietnam. They cultivate rice and are good fishermen. They have their own language, the genesis and category of which is yet to be identified, but many of them now speak Cantonese rather than or in addition to their own language. They are descended from people who migrated from Vietnam from the fifteenth century on.

JINGPO: population - 93,000, distribution - Yunnan. A group living in the extreme west of the province along the Burma border.

123

JTU: population - 159,400, distribution - Qinghai. Originally pastoralists, the Tu have practised agriculture for several centuries now. Most believe in lama Buddhism and their territory contains over forty temples. However, there are still adherents of the original polytheistic beliefs of the days before the introduction of lama Buddhism.

JUNO: population - 12,000, distribution - Yunnan. As subsistence farmers, renowned for their fine colourful fabrics, they live close to the Burma and Laos borders, in scattered mountain villages. The earliest Chinese records about them date from the eighteenth century; they are also the latest to be classified as their own separate nationality (1979). Their traditional religion is nature and ancestor worship.

KAZAKH: population - 907,600, distribution - Xinjiang, Gansu and Qinghai. Renowned for their horsemanship, the Kazakhs mainly live on the far northern plains of Xinjiang and in the Altai Mountains. They keep Bactrian camels and are wandering herders of goats and sheep. During the winter they live in communes. They are mainly Moslems, but shamanism still survives among them.

KIRGHIZ: population - 114,000, distribution - Xinjiang, Heilongjiang. As herders of goats and sheep, they are pastoral wanderers mainly living in the far west of Xinjiang bordering with the USSR. They are a Turkic people, who speak a Turkic language. Most are Islamic, although a few adhere to lama Buddhism.

KOREAN: population - 1,763,870, distri-

bution - Jilin, Liaoning and Heilongjiang. The migration of some of the Koreans into Manchuria dates from the nineteenth century. Some sources say that a very serious famine in northern Korea in 1869 drove many people towards China. Still rice-growers, they have now joined the industrialization of China's northeast. Their culture, festivals, arts and literature are the same as their co-nationals in Korea.

LAHU: population - 304,200, distribution - Yunnan. They occupy a narrow corridor of forested land between the Wa and Dai people in the southwest, close to the Burma border. Although they have their own spoken language, most of them speak Chinese or Thai through long and close association with the Han and Dai peoples. They lacked a written script until 1957.

LI: population - 817,600, distribution - Guangdong. Natives of the mountainous regions of Hainan Island, they have a long history of rebellion against the Chinese authorities and in 1943 rose against the Nationalist occupiers of their island in the first large-scale collaboration of a minority during the civil war.

LISU: population - 481,000, distribution - Yunnan, in the far west along the Burma border, and Sichuan. They are subsistence farmers. Like many of the nationalities of the southwest, their marriage system is one-man, one-wife, with marriages arranged by parents, but with rather free love before marriage.

LUOBA: population - 2,100, distribution - Tibet. The Luoba share India's northern border region with the Menba mountain herders. A record claims that they submitted to the Tibetan king in the seventh century. They speak a Tibetan language, but do not have their own script. Their traditional religion is nature worship.

MANCHU: population - 4,299,200, distribution - Liaoning, Jilin, Heilongjiang, Hebei, Beijing, Inner Mongolia and other places. Once herders and hunters, they conquered China in the seventeenth century, but though its rulers adopted Chinese manners and culture to such an extent that little now survives of their language and distinctive culture. They are found across much of northern China, working in all trades, but are among the least concentrated of all the minorities in terms of territory.

MAONAN: population - 38,100, distribution - Guangxi. Sharing a love for festivals and colourful dress with the Zhuang, they speak a related language and are excellent farmers and grow millet and buckwheat.

MENBA: population- 6,200, distribution - Tibet. Bordering India, the Menba are mountain herders, sharing a way of life not unlike that of the Tibetans, including adherence to lama Buddhism. There is a record from as early of the ninth century of their having sent tribute to, and taken orders from, the Tibetan king.

MIAO: population - 5,030,400, distribution - Guizhou, Hunan, Yunnan, Guangxi, Sichuan, Hubei and Guangdong. Among the most ancient in origin of all China's nationalities, the Miao have an identifiable history dating back some 4,000 years. They may well have had a matriarchal society at one time. Prior to modernization of their farming methods, they grew millet and buck-

wheat by the slash-and-burn method, their diet supplemented by hunting game and domestic animals. Their language has three main dialects, but there was no unified written script until 1956, when one was created for them based on Roman letters.

MONGOLIAN: population - 3,411,700,* distribution - Inner Mongolia, Xinjiang, Liaoning, Jilin, Heilongjiang, Gansu and Qinghai. The Mongolians once ran a gigantic empire, founded in 1206 by Chinggis Khan, which came to cover most of the Eurasian continent. The Mongolian script, which is still in use in the People's Republic of China, dates from the thirteenth century, based on the Uygur writing system of that time. Traditionally the Mongolians were nomadic, following their flocks of livestock to summer pastures, and covering vast distances. To this day some remain nomadic, and live in hide and felt tents called yurts. However, more and more Mongolians have taken up fixed dwellings and many now live in cities. Industry is well developed among them. Iron, coal, steel, salt, grain and livestock are important commodities.
(* Population figures for the following text are for 1982.)

MULAM: population - 90,400, distribution - Guangxi. They are an agricultural people with a self-sufficient village economy. Their religion is polytheistic and they practise ancestor worship. Their language is closely related to that of the Zhuang and many of the people speak Zhuang or Chinese. Lacking their own written language they use Chinese characters.

NAXI: population - 245,200, distribution - Yunnan, Sichuan. Though most Naxi follow a patriarchal family system, there is one section which is matriarchal.

NU: population - 23,200, distribution - Yunnan. Living along the Nu (Salween) River in the mountains of Yunnan's far west in four small pockets close to the Burma border, they are farmers and are closely related to the Tibetans. Some have accepted lama Buddhism, but others are nature-worshippers or Christians.

OROQEN: population - 4,100, distribution - Inner Mongolia and Heilongjiang. The Oroqen are a Tungus people, speaking a Tungus language. They are first mentioned in Chinese records in the middle of the seventeenth century. Once semi-nomadic, these birch and hide tent dwellers of the northeast are now living a more settled life. However, they are still great hunters, herders of deer and farmers.

PUMI: population - 24,200, distribution - Yunnan. As herders their settlements are in the mountains between the Mekong and Yangtze rivers. They speak a language related to Tibetan, and live a life similar to the Tibetans, but only a part of the nationality accepts lama Buddhism, the others have a polytheistic religion and sacrifice to their ancestors.

QIANG: population - 102,800, distribution - Sichuan. Closely-related to the Tibetans they speak a similar language, and are herders or farmers, but are polytheists, nature-worshippers, and shamanists, not lama Buddhists.

RUSSIAN: population - 2,900, distribution - Xinjiang, Heilongjiang. They consist of the two small settlements in the arid northwest, some forty kilometres from the USSR border, and a third group who have settled 600 kilometres further to the east. There is also a tiny community in China's northeast. The Chinese Russian community dates from the eighteenth century.

SALA: population - 69,100, distribution - Qinghai and Gansu. A small pocket of Islamic Turkic speakers living in the extreme east of Qinghai on the Gansu border, who, in a semi-desert area, are herders of sheep and some cattle.

SHE: population - 368,800, distribution, Fujian, Zhejiang, Jiangxi and Guangdong. They now live in small, scattered groups, mainly in Fujian Province, in the north bordering Zhejiang. Their traditional language belongs to the Miao-Yao family. Their origins are extremely unclear, but there were probably already She communities living in the mountain regions of Fujian, Guangdong and Jiangxi by the seventh century.

SHUI: population - 286,500, distribution - Guizhou, Guangxi. They occupy a very small area in the south of Guizhou Province, not far from the Dong people. Their language is close to that of the Dong.

TAJIK: population - 26,500, distribution - Xinjiang. Of Iranian stock, they speak an Iranian language and believe in Islam. They inhabit the arid far west adjoining the Pakistan, Afghanistan and USSR borders. By means of extensive irrigation, they grow rice, wheat, fruit and cotton.

TARTAR: population, 4,100, distribution - Xinjiang. Consisting of two small scattered groups of Islamic Turkic speakers, they live in the desolate far northwest as farmers.

TIBETAN: population - 3,870,100, distribution - Tibet, Qinghai, Sichuan, Gansu and Yunnan. Farmers of barley, peas and tubers, and herders of yaks, sheep and goats, the Tibetans inhabit a high desolate region in the southwest and are surrounded by mountains. They ran a powerful independent kingdom from about the fifth century until its conquest by the Mongolians in the thirteenth century, the most famous of the kings being Srong-bstan sgam-po (d. 650). Prior to the implementation of "democratic reforms" in 1959, Tibet had been a theocratic state based on Buddhism. Serfdom has since been abolished and mechanized agriculture and other modernization programs have begun. The Tibetans have a very distinctive culture, mainly based on lama Buddhism, which has produced some of the largest and most beautiful religious buildings in the world. Among China's minority nationalities they are the only one to have created an ancient tradition of drama independently of the Han people.

TUJIA: population - 2,832,700, distribution - Hunan, Hubei and Sichuan. Recognised as a minority only in the 1950s, they farm rice and corn, collect fruit and fell trees for lumber; they also produce an oil from tea and are good at handcrafts. They are in most respects very similar to the Han people.

UYGUR: population - 5,957,100, distribution - Xinjiang in the northwest, but with a small community in Hunan. The Uygurs are a Turkic people. Through the deserts and mountains of Xinjiang trade was established in the west via the fa-

mous Silk Road, which eventually allowed Islam to expand in the east. The Uygurs ran a major empire centred on what is now Mongolia from 744 to 840. They became Manichees in the eighth century, during the time of their empire, and then Buddhist. A small part of their community began to adopt Islam from the tenth century, but the process of total conversion to that religion took several centuries. The Uygurs grow fruit, wheat, cotton and rice by means of extensive systems of irrigation. Their culture, customs and arts are similar to those of other Turkic peoples. They excel in music, song and dance, their most famous musical creation being the Twelve Mukams .

UZBECK: population - 12,500, distribution - Xinjiang. A small group of well-scattered Islamic Turkic speakers living in the arid lands west of the Tarim Basin as farmers. The nationality can be dated to a fourteenth-century khanate.

VA: population - 298,600, distribution - Yunnan in the southwest bordering Burma. They speak a Mon-Khmer South Asian language. By religion they are nature-worshippers, which in the past involved them in a great deal of blood sacrifices, of chickens, pigs, cattle and even human beings.

XIBO: population - 83,600, distribution - Xinjiang, Liaoning and Jilin. Traditionally the Xibo lived in the far northeast of Liaoning with the Manchus, but in 1764 many were moved to the west as border guards on the Russian frontier of Xinjiang where they now live on the northern slopes of the Tlianshan.

YAO: population - 1,402,700, distribution - Guangxi, Hunan, Yunnan, Guang-dong and Guizhou. Living in small fenced villages scattered in the rugged mountains, they farm sweet potatoes, maize and rice, and have developed a new economy based on hydroelectric power and increased irrigation. The Yao have several different mutually incom-prehensible languages, spoken among various of their groups, and for this rea-son they often use Chinese or Zhuang as languages of communication. Their tra-ditional religions include nature wor-ship, ancestor worship, and Daoism.

YI: population - 5,453,500, distribution - Yunnan, Sichuan, Guizhou and Guangxi. At one time the Yi had the reputation as fierce warriors and devel-oped a society of 'nobility'. That portion of the Yi people living in the Liang Mountains area of southern Sichuan developed a stratified slave system in which high-level slaves themselves owned slaves. The Yi are polytheists, and Buddhism also has a long tradition among them.

YUGUR: population - 10,600, distribu-tion - Gansu. These Turkic speakers are herders and farmers living on the border with Qinghai. They are descended from one of the Uygur kingdoms which arose on the ashes of the great Uygur empire of 744 to 840. However, most of them prac-tise lama Buddhism.

ZHUANG: population - 13,378,200, distribution - Guangxi, Yunnan and Guangdong. The Zhuang are the most populous of China's minority nationali-ties, and also one of the best integrated with the Han. There is evidence that they used their own script, based on Chinese characters, about a thousand years ago.

However, it appears to have fallen into disuse, so in 1955 a new script based on Roman letters was devised. They used bronze instruments long before the time of Christ, and bronze drums from about that time have been unearthed in their territory.

BIBLIOGRAPHY

Baoerhan and others (comp.): Zhongguo da baike quanshu, minzu (China Encyclopedia, Nationalities). Beijing, Shanghai: Zhongguo da baike quanshu chubanshe. 1986.

Chen Yongling and others (comp.): Minzu cidian (Nationalities Dictionary). Shanghai: Shanghai cishu chubanshe. 1987.

China Daily.

China Handbook 1937-1944, A Comprehensive Survey of Major Developments in China in Seven Years of War. Chungking: Chinese Ministry of Information. 1944.

Chugoku Kyosanto shi shiryo shu (Collection of Documents on the History of the Chinese Communist Party). 12 vols. Tokyo: Keiso shobo, 1970-1975. Abbreviation: CK.

Chugoku shosu minzoku no kabu to gakki (The Songs and Dances and Musical Instruments of China's Minority Nationalities), Beijing: Minzu chubanshe, Tokyo: Minomi. 1981.

Dessaint, Alain Y.: Minorities of Southwest China, An Introduction to the Yi (Lolo) and Related Peoples and an Annotated Bibliography. New Haven: HRAF Press. 1980.

Dong Sen, comp.: Minjian qingge (Folk Love Songs). Beijing: Zhongguo minjian wenyi chubanshe. 1981.

Dreyer, June: China's Forty Millions, Minority Nationalities and National Integration in the People's Republic of China, Harvard East Asian Series 87. Cambridge, Mass. and London: Harvard University Press, 1976.

Eberhard, Wolfram, trans. from German by **Alide Eberhard**: The Local Cultures of South and East China. Leiden: Brill. 1968.

Epstein, Israel: Tibet Transformed. Beijing: New World Press. 1983.

Fei Hsiao Tung: Toward a People's Anthropology. Beijing: New World Press. 1981.

Gelder, Stuart and **Roma**: The Timely Rain, Travels in New Tibet. London: Hutchinson. 1964.

Grunfeld, A. Tom: In search of equality: relations between China's ethnic minorities and the majority Han. Bulletin of Concerned Asian Scholars, 17(1): 54-67. 1985.

— The Making of Modern Tibet. London: Zed Books, New York: M.E. Sharpe. 1987.

He Yun and others: Miaozu min'ge (Folksongs of the Miao Nationality), Zhongguo yinyue yanjiusuo congkan (Series of the Chinese Music Research Institute). Beijing: Yinyue chubanshe. 1959.

Heberer, Thomas: Nationalitätenpolitik und Entwicklungspolitik in den Gebieten nationaler Minderheiten in China, Bremer Beiträge zur Geographie und Raumplanung, Heft 9. Bremen: Universität Bremen. 1984.

Heissig, Walter, trans. from German by **D.J.S. Thomson**: A Lost Civilization, The Mongols Rediscovered. London: Thames and Hudson, 1966.

Hsieh, J.: China's Nationalities Policy: Its Development and Problems. Anthropos, 81: 1-20. 1986.

Israeli, Raphael: Muslims in China, A Study in Cultural Confrontation, Scandinavian Institute of Asian Studies Monograph Series No. 29. London and Malmö: Curzon Press. 1980.

Ito Seiji: Nihon shinwa to Chugoku shinwa (Japanese Myths and Chinese Myths). Tokyo: Gakusei sha. 1978.

Jagchid, Sechin and **Hyer, Paul**: Mongolia's Culture and Society. Boulder: Westview Press. 1979.

Kheir, A.M.: On Chinese Muslim customs. Hemisphere, An Asian-Australian Magazine, 28(5): 273-278. 1984.

Lattimore, Owen: Pivot of Asia, Sinkiang and the Inner Frontiers of China and Russia. Boston: Little, Brown and Company. 1950; New York: AMS Press. 1975.

— Inner Asian Frontiers of China. Boston: Beacon Press. 1962.

Lee Chae-Jin: China's Korean Minority: The Politics of Ethnic Education. Boulder and London: Westview Press. 1986.

Li Yongzeng: Education among minority peoples. Beijing Review, 26(42): 16-23. 1983.

Li Zixian: Nanfang shaoshu minzu shishi de leixing (Types of historical poems of the southern minority nationalities). Minzu wenhua (Nationalities' Cultures), 1: 6-8. 1984.

Luo Zhufeng and others (comp.): Zhongguo da baike quanshu, zongjiao (China Encyclopedia, Religion). Beijing, Shanghai: Zhongguo da baike quanshu chubanshe. 1988.

Mackerras, Colin: Aspects of Bai culture: change and continuity in a Yunnan nationality. Modern China. An International Quarterly of History and Social Science, 14(1): 51-84. 1988.

— Folksongs and dances of China's minority nationalities, policy, tradition, and professionalization. Modern China. An International Quarterly of History and Social Science, 10(2): 187-226. 1984.

— The minority nationalities: modernisation and integration. In China, Dilemmas of Modernisation, edited by Graham Young: 237-266 London: Croom Helm. 1985.

— Traditional Uygur performing arts. Asian Music, 16(1): 29-58. 1985.

McMillen, Donald H.: Chinese Communist Power and Policy in Xinjiang 1949-1977. Boulder: Westview Press. 1979.

Mao Zedong: Selected Works of Mao Tse-tung. 5 vols. Peking: Foreign Languages Press, 1965-1977.

Moseley, George: The Consolidation of the South China Frontier. Berkeley, Los Angeles, London: University of California Press. 1973.

Mullin, Chris: Tibetan conspiracy. Far Eastern Economic Review, 89(36): 30-34. 1975.

Norbu, Dawa: Red Star over Tibet. London: Collins. 1974.

Peng Yingquan and **Yang Zhiguo**: Xizang zongjiao gaishuo (Outline of Tibetan Religion). Lhasa: Xizang Renmin chubanshe, 1983.

Qiu Pu: Elunchun ren (The Oroqens). Beijing: Minzu chubanshe. 1956, 1981.

Rao Junyu: Biaoxian Yizu gudai zhanzheng de daxing wudao: Tiaogong (A large-scale dance expressing an ancient war of the Yi nationality: Leaping Palace). Minzu wenhua (Nationalities' Cultures), 1:23-24. 1984.

Ren Qin and **Qi Llanxiu**: Guanghui de shipian, buxiu de zuopin, Menggu zu yingxiong shishi 'Jianggeer' (Glorious poem, immortal work, the heroic epic 'Jangghar' of the Mongolian nationality). Minzu tuanjie (Nationalities' Unity), 4: 34-35. 1984.

Richardson, H.E.: A Short History of Tibet. New York: Dutton. 1962.

Sauvageot, Claude and **Donzé, Marie-Ange**: Une autre Chine. Paris: Albin Michel. 1980.

Schwarz, Henry G.: The Minorities of Northern China, A Survey. Bellingham, Washington: Centre for East Asian Studies, Western Washington University. 1984.

— The treatment of minorities. In China's Developmental Experience, edited by Michel Oksenberg: 193-207 New York: Praeger. 1973.

Snellgrove, David and **Richardson, Hugh**: A Cultural History of Tibet. London: George Weidenfeld and Nicholson. 1968.

Snow, Edgar: The Other Side of the River, Red China Today. New York: Random House. 1961.

— Red Star over China. Harmondsworth: Penguin, 1972 ed.

Songshi (History of the Song), 1345. Sibu beiyao edition, Shanghai: Zhonghua shuju. n.d.

Wang Duanyu: Lama jiao yu Zangzu renkou (Lamaism and the population of the Tibetan nationality). Minzu yanjiu (Nationalities Studies), 2: 44-55. 1984.

Wang Guodong: Minzu wenti changshi (General Knowledge on Nationalities Problems). Yinchuan: Ningxia Renmin chubanshe. 1982.

Wang Jun: The Juno nationality of Yunnan and their village communes. Social Sciences in China 3(4): 84-105. 1982.

Wang Kefen: Zhongguo gudai wudao shihua (History of Ancient Chinese Dance), Wudao zhishi congshu (Dance

Knowledge Series), Beijing: Renmin yinyue chubanshe. 1980.

—, trans. from Chinese **Ke Ruibo**: The History of Chinese Dance. Beijing: Foreign Languages Press. 1985.

Winnington, Alan: The Slaves of the Cool Mountains. London: Lawrence and Wishart. 1959.

Wong How-man: Peoples of China's far provinces. National Geographic, 165(3): 283-333. 1984.

Yan Ruxian: A living fossil of the family - A study of the family structure of the Naxi nationality in the Lugu Lake region. Social Sciences in China 3(4): 60-83. 1982.

Yanbian Chaoxian zu zizhi zhou gaikuang (Survey of the Yanbian Korean Nationality Autonomous Prefecture), Zhongguo shaoshu minzu zizhi difang gaikuang congshu (Series of Surveys on the Autonomous Places of China's Minority Nationalities). Yanji: Yanbian Renmin chubanshe. 1984.

Yaozu jianshi (Brief History of the Yao Nationality), Zhongguo shaoshu minzu jianshi congshu (Series of Brief Histories of China's Minority Nationalities). Nanning: Guangxi Minzu chubanshe. 1983.

Yin Ming: United and Equal, The Progress of China's Minority Nationalities. Peking: Foreign Languages Press. 1977.

Yuan Bingchang, Mao Jizeng, and others: Zhongguo shaoshu minzu yueqi zhi (Musical Instruments of China's Minority Nationalities). Beijing: Xin shijie chubanshe. 1986.

Zhang Geng and others (comp.): Zhongguo da baike quanshu, xiqu quyi (China Encyclopedia, Theatre and Balladry). Beijing, Shanghai: Zhongguo da baike quanshu chubanshe. 1983.

Zhang Tianlu: Growth of China's minority population. Beijing Review 27(25): 22-26, 30. 1984.

Zhongguo min'ge xuan (Selection of Chinese Folksongs). Beijing: Renmin yinyue chubanshe. 1980. Abbreviation: ZMX.

Zhongguo minzu guanxi shi lunwen ji (Collection of Papers on the History of Relations Among China's Nationalities). 2 vols. Beijing: Minzu chubanshe. 1982.

Zhongguo shaoshu minzu (China's Minority Nationalities). Beijing: Renmin chubanshe. 1981. Abbreviation: ZSM.

Zhongguo tongji nianjian 1986 (Chinese Statistical Yearbook 1986). Beijing.

Zhongguo tongji chubanshe. 1986. Abbreviation: ZTN.

INDEX